# NOTE

Some recent developments in the National Seashore—including new facilities and regulations—are discussed the the supplements beginning on p. 115.

# POINT REYES

A Guide to the Trails,
Roads, Beaches,
Campgrounds, Lakes,
Trees, Flowers and Rocks
of Point Reyes
National Seashore

Dorothy L. Whitnah

Wilderness
Press

Photography and design are by Luther Linkhart. Flower drawings
are by Jeanne R. Janish, and are used courtesy of the University of
California Press. Maps are by Jeffrey P. Schaffer.

# ACKNOWLEDGMENTS

I am grateful to the following persons, who have provided companionship, hospitality, information, refreshments, and advice (which I have not always taken):

Robert D. Bardell
Richard A. Brown
Katherine Clark
D. Steven Corey
Richard H. Dillon
Marge and Phil Drath
Gordon and Mary Griffiths
James D. Hart
Stephen Gale Herrick
Serena Jutkovitz
Gaye L. Kelly
Noelle Liebrenz
Luther and Virginia Linkhart
Don Neubacher of the National Park
  Service
Arlen and Clare Philpott
Will Powers
David Pugh of the National Park
  Service
George F. Ritchie
Madeleine S. Rose
Emily and Julia Ross
Shirley Sheffield
Diana Skiles of the National Park
  Service
Ann and Gregory Whipple
Caroline, Jason, Lucille and Thomas
  Winnett
Malcolm Yorke

First edition 1981
Second edition 1985
Second printing May 1987
Third printing December 1988
Fourth printing January 1991

Library of Congress Card Catalog
Number 85-051088

International Standard Book Number
0-89997-056-7

Manufactured in the United States

Published by Wilderness Press
    2440 Bancroft Way
    Berkeley, CA 94704

(415) 843-8080

Write for free catalog

**Library of Congress Cataloging-in-Publication Data**

Whitnah, Dorothy L.
    Point Reyes : a guide to the trails, roads, beaches, campgrounds, lakes, trees, flowers, and rocks of Point Reyes National Seashore.

    Includes index.
    1. Point Reyes National Seashore (Calif.)--Guidebooks. I. Title.
F868.P9W47   1985        917.94'62        85-51088
ISBN 0-89997-056-7 (pbk.)

# CONTENTS

Alamere Falls cascades to the sea
near the southern end
of Wildcat Beach

# PREFACE

One day in 1972 I walked along a beach. It was at Scheveningen, Holland, but it might have been at any popular seaside resort near a metropolis almost anywhere in the Western World—Brighton, Ostia, Jones Beach, Laguna Beach. Children frolicked in the surf and built sandcastles just beyond the reach of the waves; adults sunbathed on the warm sand and strolled along the boardwalk lined with cafes, restaurants, hotels, stores of all kinds. An urbane, civilized setting, I mused—a pleasant spot for citizens of an industrial society to enjoy their leisure.

Suddenly a pang of homesickness rushed through me, a yearning for the long windswept beaches of my youth, where one could often walk for miles without seeing another human being, and the nearest reminder of civilization might be a piece of lumber washed up on the sand, or a Japanese glass float. Along with the homesickness, however, went a profound feeling of relief and gratitude that such a wild beach still exists, only 50 miles from my home—and, God willing, will continue to exist indefinitely in its present state.

And not only a long, wild beach, but also sheltered, quiet beaches, and deep, mysterious forests, and pastoral meadows echoing with birdsong.

Do we of the San Francisco metropolitan area truly appreciate the near-miracle of the 65,000-acre Point Reyes National Seashore just an hour away from our homes? We came within a hair's breadth of getting Jones Beach West instead.

I call it a near-miracle; but in addition to providence, it took a lot of hard work. We all owe thanks to those dedicated Marin County conservationists who must have frequently felt that they were engaged in a labor of Sisyphus as they tried to save for the public, in perpetuity, land that was escalating in value 10 to 20 per cent each year. Most of all, we owe a debt of gratitude to five legislators: the late Senator Clair Engle and the late Representatives Clem Miller and Phillip Burton, plus Phillip's brother John, former Representative in Congress of Marin County, and Barbara Boxer, Marin's current Representative.

The best tribute we can pay their devoted efforts is to use our National Seashore, enjoy it and cherish it.

**Walking beside the rugged cliffs
near Sculptured Beach
at low tide**

# INTRODUCTION

The Point Reyes peninsula is a place of great fascination for geologists. You can easily see why when you walk along the short Earthquake Trail near park headquarters (see p. 31), which runs along the San Andreas fault zone. This landscape dramatically illustrates the new geology: the concept of plate tectonics.

To summarize this concept briefly:

The outer layer of the earth, the *lithosphere*, is composed of huge, contiguous crustal plates, about 60 miles thick. These plates are gliding over the *asthenosphere*, a hot, molten layer about 200 miles thick. In some places, two plates meet head on, and one overrides the other, the lower plate diving into the asthenosphere, where it melts (see the figure below).

In other places, two plates move away from each other. But instead of a fissure developing between them, a ridge develops. This ridge is formed of molten material that comes from beneath the earth's crust and erupts onto the ocean floor (see the figure). In yet other places, two plates glide horizontally past each other. That's what's happening in the San Andreas fault zone, which represents the boundary between the Pacific plate to the west and the North American plate to the east.

The primeval North American continent was originally part of a single supercontinent, which also included primeval Eurasia, Africa, South America and Antarctica. Roughly 230 million years ago the pieces of this supercontinent began to drift apart and the North American plate began to override the Pacific plate. For 200 million years the North American plate moved westward, carrying the primeval North American continent atop it. Then, about 30 million years ago, these two plates began to slip laterally past each other. This slippage is still going on, and we call the interface between the two slipping plates the San Andreas fault zone.

At present the Pacific plate is moving northwest relative to the North American plate at slightly more than 2 inches a year. If this rate had been steady for the entire 30 million years since lateral movement began, total displacement along the fault would have been 1100 miles—a figure most geologists consider too high. Correlation of similar rock samples on the two sides of the fault suggests a movement of something over 300 miles.

Although the Pacific plate is generally moving northwest an estimated 2 inches per year, we know that on April 18, 1906, it moved as much as twenty feet in just a few moments. Maximum displacement occurred not in San Francisco but in the Olema Valley, just outside what is now the National Seashore.

Certainly the San Andreas fault is the most significant—indeed, the determining—feature of the Point Reyes peninsula's general shape. The segment of the fault we are here concerned with runs southwest under

Plate tectonics

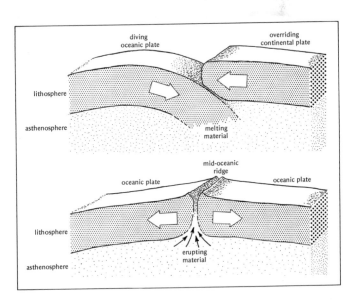

Tomales Bay, and continues through the Olema Valley (the route of State Highway 1) and under Bolinas Lagoon. The bedrock of the peninsula—granite about 80 million years old—is entirely different from the rock east of the fault, which is rock of the Franciscan Formation—a jumble of mainly sedimentary rocks laid down 100–150 million years ago.

# TOPOGRAPHY

The most prominent feature the visitor will notice is densely forested Inverness Ridge, which runs northwest along the peninsula, parallel to the fault zone. Its highest point is Mt. Wittenberg, 1407 feet—a fairly short, scenic climb from park headquarters. On the east, the ridge descends steeply to pastoral Olema Valley; on the west, it descends more gently to rolling pastures and the drowned river valleys and sheltered beaches of Drakes and Limantour esteros.

To the northwest, between the ocean and Tomales Bay, lie more pastures and windswept moors that have reminded visitors of Yorkshire or Scotland. At the southwestern tip of the peninsula, the rocky promontory of Point Reyes rises 600 feet above the pounding surf. And along the western edge lie miles of white sandy beach—beautiful but wild.

Even casual hikers, bicyclists and equestrians on the Point Reyes peninsula will notice evidence of the area's unique geology. As you wander along the trails, streams change course abruptly; fresh-water lakes appear in unexpected places; landslides are apparent; and as you picnic on the beach you can watch the cliffs eroding before your eyes (in fact, if you sit too close to them you can actually feel them eroding, as sand and pebbles shower down onto your head and into your drinking cup).

We shall note some of these phenomena as we explore the trails.

Studying the seismic map at park headquarters in Bear Valley

### Recommended reading

Galloway, Alan J., *Geology of the Point Reyes Peninsula, Marin County, California.* Sacramento: California Division of Mines and Geology, 1977. Bulletin 202. Paperback. Includes bibliography and elaborate map; usually available at park headquarters.

Galloway, Alan J., *Guide to Point Reyes Peninsula and the San Andreas Fault Zone.* San Francisco: California Division of Mines and Geology, 1966. Paperback. This is Field Trip A from the division's Bulletin #190: an auto itinerary from San Francisco up Highway 1 to Point Reyes, returning by Sir Francis Drake Highway.

Like the rest of the Bay Area, Point Reyes has what is called a Mediterranean climate, characterized by a wet season (roughly October–March) and a dry (roughly April–September). However, the peninsula gets a lot more summer fog than most areas of Mediterranean climate, including some other parts of Marin County. Proponents of Drakes Bay as the great navigator's California landing place put forth as one of their main arguments his annalist's kvetching about the weather: " . . . notwithstanding it was in the height of Summer, and so near the Sun; yet were we continually visited with . . . nipping colds . . . neither could we at any time in the whole fourteen days together, find the air so clear as to be able to take the height of Sun or star . . ." He complained also about the "thick mists and most stinking fogs."

What this means for the modern visitor is: come prepared for cool weather even in mid-summer; bring a sweater or windbreaker, or both. Bear in mind also that the weather frequently varies *within* the park: for example, the beaches may be fogged in while the Olema area enjoys brilliant sunshine. You can phone headquarters (663-1092) in advance to find out what the weather is like.

Because the rocks of the Point Reyes peninsula differ so markedly from those to the east of the fault zone, it follows that the soils differ also; so it comes as no surprise that the peninsula's plant life differs from that of the mainland.

The majestic Black Forest of Douglas fir on Inverness Ridge is awesomely impressive. John Thomas Howell, the pre-eminent Marin botanist, believes it resembles the dense fir forests of the Pacific Northwest more closely than it does the nearby ones. Another noteworthy conifer is the bishop pine, the only pine native to Marin County. (You will find other pine trees growing in the county—in particular, Monterey pine—but they or their seeds originally came from somewhere else.) Although the bishop occurs sparsely elsewhere in Marin, there are large groves of it on the north end of Inverness Ridge. It is a closed-cone pine: the cones open only after a fire to reseed the forest.

Interestingly enough, the coast redwood, which plays such a prominent arboreal role on the east side of the fault zone, is not found on the Point Reyes peninsula. Apparently coast redwoods do not favor granitic soil.

Towering Douglas firs and bay (California laurel) trees line the Sky Trail on the way to Mt. Wittenberg

13

Graceful alders line a stream bank

Pussy's ears, or hairy star tulip, flowers in the meadows in spring

Douglas iris abounds in the National Seashore

The one plant you must be able to recognize: poison oak

Other trees that occur in association with the Douglas firs and bishop pines are such common central California natives as the coast live oak, the bay, the madrone and the buckeye.

Your walks in the National Seashore will take you to many kinds of landscapes other than forests: grassy meadows; coastal scrub (also called soft chaparral); marshes, both fresh-water and salt-water; and of course miles of beach and dune. Each of these has its own plant community, and a few of the plants are found only on the Point Reyes peninsula.

From about February through June, all of the landscapes are brightened by the blooming of wildflowers. In the forest the delicate white milkmaids herald the coming of spring. On the coastal bluffs the baby-blue-eyes, pale suncups, shiny buttercups and elegant iris form a living Oriental carpet thrown over the land. And everywhere the variously colored lupine and the golden California poppy (our state flower) enliven the roadsides.

One plant the Point Reyes peninsula has, alas, in common with much of the rest of northern California—poison oak. It is easy to avoid on the broad and well-traveled trails like Bear Valley, but on narrower and less-frequented trails one should remain alert for the distinctive leaves in groups of three that are glossy green in spring and brilliant red in late summer and fall. It is especially sneaky when encountered as a vine at head level above the trail, often camouflaged by other, harmless plants. If you try going cross-country or on unmaintained trails in brushy areas, be prepared to run into lots of poison oak, and dress accordingly: long pants and long sleeves.

Drawings of some of the common flowers of Point Reyes are at the end of this book.

### Recommended reading

Ferris, Roxana S., *Flowers of Point Reyes National Seashore.* Berkeley, Los Angeles and London: University of California Press, 1970. Illustrated by Jeanne R. Janish. Paperback.

Howell, John Thomas, *Marin Flora.* 2nd ed. Berkeley and Los Angeles: University of California Press, 1970. Photographs by Charles T. Townsend. The definitive guide to the county's plants.

## Birds

The Point Reyes peninsula is a favored haunt of birders, boasting as it does 338 recorded species. This avian abundance is due partly to the diversity of its habitats—forest, pasture, seashore, marshland, all in close proximity—and partly to its coastal location, which attracts many wintering migrants.

You can pick up a checklist of birds for 75¢ at headquarters. Serious birders will want to visit the Point Reyes Bird Observatory (see p. 84).

For the casual visitor, perhaps the most exciting bird-oriented activity is watching hawks perched on the fences and telephone poles along the outer stretches of Sir Francis Drake Highway and Pierce Point Road. You can get surprisingly close to these birds, and I have seen drivers almost go off the road when fascinated by a majestic marsh hawk alighting nearby.

## Land Animals

It is evident from travelers' reports that game was once abundant on the peninsula. Drake's annalist remarked on the "herds of wild deer" and the "multitude of a strange kind of Conies," with bags under their chin on either side, which the crew of the *Golden Hinde* encountered. The "deer" were probably tule elk. The "Conies" are somewhat harder to identify with certainty and have burrowed their way into the ongoing Drake controversy. Proponents of Drakes Bay as the *Golden Hinde's* harbor claim they were pocket gophers, which are indeed multitudinous on the Point Reyes peninsula; proponents of other bays claim they were ground squirrels.

The vaqueros of the early 19th century hunted deer and elk that roamed the peninsula in huge herds. As late as the 1890s the sportsmen of the Pacific Union Club were hunting coyote, bear and mountain lion, as well as deer and elk, in Bear Valley. The bear are gone now, and the occasional coyote and mountain lion is seen only by the remarkably fortunate and sharpsighted. The last of the Point Reyes tule elk were slaughtered for their meat and hides in the 1860s—unless, as one report had it, they swam to safety across Tomales Bay. In 1978 the National Park Service reintroduced a small herd transported from the Owens Valley in Southern California. The elk are fenced off in 2600 acres on the northern part of Tomales Point, and as of this writing are flourishing and reproducing.

Cormorants nest on the secluded cliffs near Miller Point

Tule elk have been re-established in their original habitat on Tomales Point

Other mammals whose tracks, scats or burrows you may see include skunks, foxes, bobcats, gophers, weasels and rabbits. Point Reyes is also the southern limit of the range of a burrowing animal, the aplodontia (called "mountain beaver," although it is not a beaver), which is so reclusive that it is rarely encountered. An animal you are only too likely to encounter if you are backpacking is the raccoon, which will try to steal your food unless you hang it carefully on the poles provided at the campsites.

It is almost impossible to hike for an hour or so on Point Reyes without seeing a deer. In addition to the native black-tailed deer, the peninsula contains two exotic species: the white-to-brown fallow deer, native to the Mediterranean lands and Asia Minor, and the spotted axis deer, native to India and Ceylon. Both species were introduced to the peninsula in the 1940s and '50s by ranch-owner Dr. Millard Ottinger. The exotic deer flourished in their new habitat, and the herds increased from a few dozen to the hundreds. The three species coexist peacefully but do not interbreed. Ranchers occasionally hunted deer on their own lands, but when the National Seashore was established hunting was forbidden. The problem of controlling the exotic deer population explosion is a thorny one for the park service. Obviously the herds cannot be allowed to multiply exponentially, yet any proposal to thin their number meets opposition. Meanwhile the exotic deer, especially the white ones, contribute one of the most striking embellishments to outings in the National Seashore.

Because many ranchers have long-term leases, hikers will continue to see dairy cattle, and even a few goats around Abbotts Lagoon.

## Aquatic Animals

Harbor seals are frequently seen and heard in the esteros and Tomales Bay, and sea lions on the rocks off the coast. By far the most spectacular marine mammals visible in the National Seashore, however, are not residents but migrants: the California gray whales that travel down from Alaska to Baja California every winter to bear their young, returning north in spring. These magnificent animals often pass within a few hundred yards of the coast. On a clear day the lucky visitor may see dozens of whales, and may even see them "breach"—leap out of the water as high as 30 feet.

The best places to watch the whales are from the lighthouse area and the western cliffs and beaches. Whale watching has become so popular that in the winter of 1979–80 the park instituted a free shuttle bus between Drakes Beach and the lighthouse to avoid traffic jams on the narrow road. To find out in advance about weather conditions, whale activity, traffic, etc., you can call Bear Valley headquarters (663-1092) or the lighthouse visitor center (669-1534). The rangers distribute a free information sheet on the whales.

## Fish and Shellfish

The best way to find out about fishing possibilities and regulations in the National Seashore is to pick up a free information sheet on the subject at Bear Valley headquarters. A

White fallow deer, native to the Mediterranean, were introduced on Point Reyes by a 1940s landowner

Steller's sea lions often haul out on the ocean side of Tomales Point few pointers to bear in mind:

Persons 16 years of age or older must have in their possession a valid California state fishing license for the taking of any kind of fish, mollusk, amphibian or crustacean. (You should obtain this license *before* you come to the park.)

The surf on the ocean beaches is extremely hazardous.

Mussels are quarantined every year from May 1 to November 1 because they may be poisonous then. The poison results from shellfish consuming toxic algae, the "red tides" of summer and early fall. In the summer of 1980, for the first time in many years, this poison began showing up in clams and oysters as well as mussels. From now on, one should take care to check quarantine notices before collecting any shellfish between May and November.

Great white sharks breed in the waters off Tomales Point and have attacked skin divers in that area on several occasions.

A surf fisherman
tries his luck
at Drakes Beach

# HISTORY

The first residents of Point Reyes were Coast Miwok Indians. Archeologists have identified 113 aboriginal village sites on the peninsula; indeed, probably more people were living there in the 16th century than there are in the 20th. With bow and arrow they hunted deer, elk, bear and mountain lion. They also gathered clams and mussels, and in small canoes made of rushes they fished the bays. A peaceable people, they greeted the first European visitors—Drake and Cermeno—with friendliness.

When the Franciscan fathers established Mission San Rafael in 1817, they recruited the Point Reyes Indians, converted them, and persuaded them to take up agriculture. Many of the Indians died of the white man's diseases, particularly smallpox. When the Mexican government secularized the missions in the 1830s, the Indian proselytes were left to fend for themselves, and many starved. A culture that had existed for hundreds of years in ecological harmony with its land thus perished in only one generation. However, you can get some idea of how the Point Reyes Indians lived when you visit Kule Loklo, the newly constructed Miwok Village near park headquarters (see p. 32).

The first European to set foot on the peninsula was probably Francis Drake, in

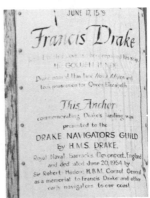

The Drake Navigators' Guild
has commemorated
the entrance to Drakes Estero,
where it believes he landed
in 1579

1579—although after 400 years debate still rages fiercely on this matter (see pp. 58-63).

The first of 40 recorded shipwrecks in the area was that of Sebastian Rodriguez Cermeno's *San Agustin* in 1595. The Portuguese captain was bringing a Manila galleon laden with luxury cargo—including silks and porcelain—from the Philippines to Acapulco. The Spanish government in Mexico had also commissioned him to explore the California coast in search of suitable harbors for the galleons. Cermeno brought the *San Agustin* into Drakes Bay to reconnoiter. (He called it the Bay of San Francisco, thereby adding to the eventual confusion attending the identification and nomenclature of the various ports along the coast.) While most of the crew was ashore, a sudden gale dashed the galleon onto the shore and wrecked her, killing several of the men. The cargo was lost; the local Indians later collected bits and pieces of the priceless Ming porcelain that washed ashore, which archaeologists subsequented discovered when they excavated Miwok villages.

Cermeno salvaged a small open launch, the *San Buenaventura*, and with his 70 remaining men and a dog set out in it for home. After a grueling voyage that represents one of the most remarkable feats of seamanship on record, they arrived safely in Mexico in January of 1596—except for the dog, which the men ate when they got desperate. Seven years later one of these survivors, Sebastian Vizcaino, sailed back up the California coast. He arrived off the peninsula on January 6, 1603, the Day of the Three Kings, and christened it *Punto de los Reyes*.

Point Reyes was part of Alta California, a Spanish colony, but the Spaniards never settled the peninsula. After Mexico threw off the Spanish yoke in 1821, the Mexican government began handing out land grants in California on a lavish scale. In 1836 James R. Berry, an Irishman who had served as a colonel in the Mexican army, was awarded about 35,000 acres on the northern part of the peninsula—Rancho Punta de los Reyes. In the same year Rafael Garcia was granted nearly 9000 acres on the southern part of the peninsula—Rancho Tomales y Baulenes. Even by the rather lax standards of land stewardship prevailing at the time, both men were remarkably casual about their holdings. Berry sold part of his land (though sale was forbidden by the terms of his grant), and hired Garcia to run cattle on part of the rest; and Garcia let his brother-in-law move into

part of *his* share. As Marin historian Jack Mason puts it: "By 1844 nobody seemed to know who owned what, and the rancheros asked Monterey [the capital of Alta California] to straighten things out. Whatever progress they may have made was wiped out in the American conquest of California in 1846." After decades of tangled litigation, most of the peninsula ended up in the hands of three lawyers from Vermont: brothers Oscar L. Shafter and James McMillan Shafter, and Charles Webb Howard, who married Oscar Shafter's daughter.

In the 1850s the Shafter-Howard clan began leasing the land for dairy farming—a use that continues to this day. Point Reyes butter was of the highest quality, and was preferred by such elegant customers as San Francisco's Palace Hotel. Schooners carrying butter and live hogs traveled once or twice a week from Drakes Estero to the City, returning with feed and grain.

A wagon road from San Rafael to Olema was completed in 1865, and thereafter a stagecoach made the trip twice a week. The town of Olema flourished, at one point boasting three hotels. James M. Shafter thought a railroad from the eastern part of the county would be a profitable venture, and he invested heavily in the North Pacific Coast Railroad. The first train ran from Sausalito to Tomales in 1875. However, far from enriching Shafter, the railroad threatened to bankrupt him. In an attempt to pay off his creditors—who included Leland Stanford and Wells Fargo—he created the town of Inverness in 1889 on 640 acres of his land on the western shore of Tomales Bay. He also envisioned an even grander development on the shore of Drakes Bay. But before these plans could come to fruition, Shafter died. His three children, especially his daughter Julia, struggled for most of their lives to pay off his debts. San Francisco's exclusive Pacific Union Club in 1895 bought 110 acres of their Bear Valley land (for $6000!) as the site of a country club. Here the cream of San Francisco male society, and such guests as Teddy Roosevelt and Ignace Paderewski, came to hunt the deer, coyote, bear and mountain lion which still inhabited the peninsula. Julia's attempt to sell her Inverness lots was thwarted by the earthquake of 1906, which severely damaged several buildings in the village.

During Prohibition, the isolated and sparsely inhabited peninsula was a natural location for extensive rum-running and bootlegging. The multitude of bay and ocean beaches and of private wharves facilitated transfer of the liquor from ships standing offshore, down from Canada. Many—probably most—of the ranchers were more sympathetic to the bootleggers than to the Prohibition agents, and looked the other way when they heard trucks roaring over the back roads at midnight.

Shortly before World War II the last of the Shafter-Howard properties was sold off. The San Francisco investor who bought Oscar's heirs' land almost immediately resold it at a profit. The Los Angeles syndicate that bought most of James Shafter's son's property announced grandiose plans for it, as had James earlier: formation of deluxe villa sites, a polo ground, a golf course, and other expensive amenities. The war put an end to these dreams, at least temporarily.

As early as 1935 the National Park Service had recommended the purchase of 53,000 acres of Point Reyes for $2.4 million, or about $45 per acre. In retrospect this seems an incredible bargain, but at that time the country was still staggering out of the Great Depression, and Congress did not throw around huge sums with such carefree abandon as it does now.

Meanwhile, Marin conservationists succeeded in having a few properties set aside as county parks: a parcel at Drakes Beach in 1938 and at McClures Beach in 1942 (both of which were subsequently taken over by the National Seashore), and the nucleus of Tomales Bay State Park in 1945.

After World War II the National Park Service began studying Point Reyes with increasingly urgent interest. For a century, various landowners and promoters had talked of exploiting this land and subdividing it for estates, but somehow their plans had always come to nothing. Now, however, loggers were actually cutting down trees on Inverness Ridge, and surveyors were actually marking off lots above Limantour Spit. At this point Marin conservationists gained a powerful ally—Clem Miller, the new Congressman from the district in which Point Reyes lay. California Senator Clair Engle also took a keen interest in the proposed park. Opposition came not only from developers but also from ranchowners who wanted to go on following their traditional

# THE MAKING OF A PARK

**The Upper Pierce Ranch buildings on Tomales Point will be maintained by the National Park Service**

way of life. Extensive negotiations made it possible for them to continue ranching on long-term leases. In 1962 President John F. Kennedy signed the Point Reyes National Seashore Bill authorizing the original 53,000 acres.

Congress, however, was niggardly in appropriating funds for purchasing the land. The original $13 million authorized ran out before half of the 53,000 acres were acquired, and as land values in Marin escalated in the following years the National Park Service was often just one jump ahead of the developers. The final cost of the park was $56 million—more than four times the amount initially budgeted. The National Park Service learned a valuable, albeit expensive, lesson from this experience.

As John Hart points out in *San Francisco's Wilderness Next Door*, the delay in completing the park led to one providential and incalculable benefit. In the early '60s most planners as well as the general public thought of parks in terms of organized and *motorized* recreation. Point Reyes National Seashore was originally planned to accommodate motor boats, dune buggies, campers, trailers, and of course thousands of cars. But by the time the last of the originally planned land was acquired in 1970, northern Californians had begun to rebel against the tyranny of the internal-combustion engine. Now they wanted to preserve the peninsula in as near its natural state as possible, as a unique heritage from the past. The only major construction that resulted from the planners' original auto-oriented outlook is the broad northern section of the Limantour Road, which was authorized along its present route in 1966. Construction within a 400-foot right-of-way in steep terrain necessitated much cut and fill, and evoked howls from environmentalists. The National Park Service's money ran out before the road could be completed on the grandiose scale originally planned, and therefore it reverts abruptly near its summit to the original narrow paving.

Another reason Point Reyes National Seashore developed differently in the 1970s than might have been expected in the early '60s is that when the Golden Gate National Recreation Area was established in 1972 it became natural to regard the peninsula as the northernmost and least developed part of a greenbelt of over 100,000 acres—an unprecedented stretch of parkland in and near a major metropolitan center. The Citizens' Advisory Commission that was established in 1972 to oversee the development of the GGNRA also looks after adjoining Point Reyes. This Commission meets regularly at various places in the Bay Area, and welcomes suggestions and opinions from the public. (To find out the schedule of meetings, phone 556-4484 or 556-0560.)

Beginning in 1975 the National Park Service held over 200 workshops among various Bay Area community groups to find out what

A row of houses once lined Limantour Spit in the background

the public wanted from the two parks. Some parts of the GGNRA, such as Alcatraz, stirred up considerable controversy; but there was general agreement that Point Reyes should be left substantially as it was.

And that is what has happened. In fact, some of the park has not only been left as it was in 1970, but is being encouraged to revert to an earlier state: in 1976 Congress designated 32,000 acres as wilderness or potential wilderness (no permanent structures or major roads, no motorized vehicles allowed except for emergencies). Another 18,000 acres are zoned for ranching on long-term lease, because the National Park Service believes that on these lands "dairying and cattle ranching are desirable aspects of the scene from both an educational and esthetic point of view." Within the park, development will proceed cautiously, and planners will listen to users' opinions before putting in more camps, hostels and parking lots.

## Recommended Reading

Arnot, Phil, *Exploring Point Reyes*. San Carlos, Wide World, Inc., 1981. Enthusiastic reminiscences of his ramblings by an energetic hiker and rock climber.

Dalbey, Alice F., *The Visitor's Guide to Point Reyes National Seashore*. Riverside, Connecticut: Chatham Press, 1974.

Doss, Margot Patterson, *Paths of Gold in and Around the Golden Gate National Recreation Area*. San Francisco: Chronicle Books, 1974. Includes 15 hikes in the National Seashore.

Gilliam, Harold, *Island in Time*. 2nd rev. ed. New York: Sierra Club/Scribner's, 1973. The classic work on the Point Reyes peninsula, with many beautiful photographs by Philip Hyde.

Hart, John, *San Francisco's Wilderness Next Door*. San Rafael and London: Presidio Press, 1979. Good account of the formation of the GGNRA and the National Seashore.

Mason, Jack, *Point Reyes, the Solemn Land*. 3rd ed. Inverness: North Shore Books, 1980. The late historian of West Marin wrote several other books, alone and in cooperation with other authors. Some relevant titles are: *Earthquake Bay: A History of Tomales Bay; Last Stage for Bolinas;* and *Summer Town: The History of Inverness, California*.

U. S. Department of the Interior, National Park Service, *Golden Gate National Recreation Area/-Point Reyes National Seashore - General Management Plan/Environmental Analysis*. 1979. Available for study at libraries and the parks' headquarters.

# TRANSIT

The park planners, both professional and amateur, have devoted an enormous amount of time and energy to the problems involved in getting *to* the park and getting around *in* it. In fact, probably no other issue (except rules governing dogs) has evoked so much emotion. The problems are more vexing in Point Reyes than in the GGNRA because the peninsula is farther from San Francisco and from most public transit.

Nearly everyone agrees that people without automobiles—as geologist Clyde Wahrhaftig puts it, "the large number of my fellow citizens who are too old, too young, too poor, or too wise to own a car"—should be able to get to the park. And the residents of the small villages adjoining the park wax vehement against widening the roads to encourage more auto traffic, or building more parking lots near their homes. And anyone who has crept south on Highway 101 toward the Golden Gate Bridge at dusk on a fair Sunday will admit that weekend traffic snarls in Marin County have already reached horrendous proportions.

Conservation activists and the park's managers have propagandized in favor or public transit, and the GGNRA–Point Reyes General Management Plan outlines several proposals relying heavily on buses and ferries.

And yet . . . so far it has seemed almost

**A solitary driver makes his way north on Highway 1 toward Olema on a frosty morning**

impossible to pry Americans out of their cars. As the park planners sum it up, the general attitude among the public is, "I want to drive there, but everyone else should take the bus." Bolinas attorney Paul Kayfetz was equally pessimistic when he testified before the Citizens' Advisory Commission in October 1979: "If we did everything possible to provide public access to the park, we would be able to, at a maximum, triple the number of visitors coming to the park in buses . . . Only 95 per cent of visitors will be coming to the park in autos, instead of 98.5 per cent."

The transportation situation may change abruptly, depending on the price and availability of gas, the funding of public transit, and other unpredictables.

## How To Get There By Bus:

Golden Gate Transit bus #65 runs on Saturdays, Sundays and holidays from San Rafael to Olema, Point Reyes National Seashore Headquarters, Point Reyes Station and Inverness. San Rafael is a major transfer point for buses from San Francisco, Sonoma County and the rest of Marin County.

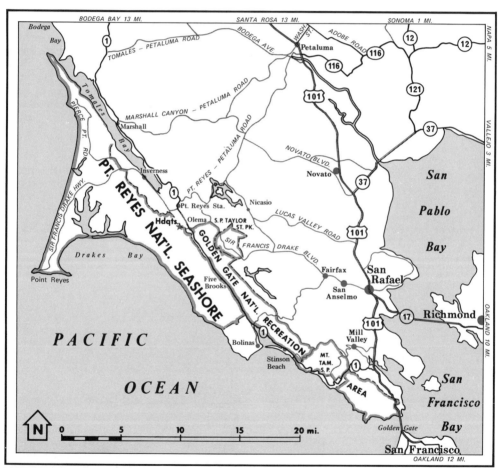

**ROADS TO THE NATIONAL SEASHORE**
MAP 1

LEGEND:

━━━━━━ Roads
‧‧‧‧‧‧ Trail
▄▄▄▄ Park Bdy.
⊙ Campground

Because the #65 runs to the Seashore in the morning and returns in the late afternoon, the bus rider can spend most of a day enjoying the park.

For information on schedules and fees, phone Golden Gate Transit:

from San Francisco, (415) 332-6600
from Marin, (415) 453-2100;
from Sonoma, (707) 544-1323.

## How To Get There By Car:

There are three principal routes to headquarters at Bear Valley. (For routes to Palomarin, the lighthouse and the various beaches, see their respective sections.) The quickest is from Highway 101 west on Sir Francis Drake Boulevard (which subsequently becomes Sir Francis Drake Highway) through Samuel P. Taylor State Park to Olema, where signs point the way to park headquarters ½ mile west. A slower, more scenic route from San Francisco or southern Marin is via winding Highway 1 north to Olema. Another scenic route is by Highway 101 and Lucas Valley Road through Nicasio to Point Reyes Station and south to Olema.

## Within The Park

On summer weekends and holidays the park used to provide free shuttle-bus service between Bear Valley headquarters and Limantour. This service was a great boon to hikers and backpackers, making possible one-way, all-downhill trips. However, first the closing of the Limantour Road because of storm

damage (see p. 49) and then the greatly reduced NPS budget have eliminated the shuttle bus.

When whale watching became such a popular activity that on weekends cars were lined up for miles along the narrow road to the lighthouse, the Park Service instituted shuttle-bus service between Drakes Beach and the lighthouse during the height of the whale migration. Alas, this service also fell victim to cuts in the NPS budget.

# FACILITIES

## Visitor Centers:

Headquarters, Bear Valley — 8 a.m.-5 p.m. weekends, 9 a.m.–5 p.m. weekdays — 663-1092

Drakes Beach — weekends and holidays 10 a.m.–4:30 p.m. — 669-1250

Lighthouse — Thursday through Monday 10 a.m.–5 p.m. (but closed when very foggy or windy.) — 669-1534

Address of all of the above: Point Reyes, CA 94956

## Picnicking

At present the only food concession in the park is at Drakes Beach, open Friday through Tuesday 11 a.m.–4:30 p.m., "weather permitting." However, several

Enjoying a snack at the Drakes Beach visitor center

towns adjoining the park have grocery stores, restaurants and delicatessens where you can purchase food for picnicking.

Next to the parking lot near headquarters is a picnic ground with tables and braziers. All the backpacking camps have picnic tables and braziers; so does Drakes Beach.

Backpackers at Wildcat Camp hang their packs on the racks provided, out of reach of raccoons

## Camping

The only overnight camping in the park is at hike-in camps for backpackers. Headquarters will provide visitors with a free list of nearby car-camping facilities. (The nearest are at Olema Ranch Campground and Samuel P. Taylor State Park.)

The four hike-in camps currently in the park contain a total of 38 family campsites and 12 group campsites. They present a golden opportunity to the novice backpacker or the family that wants to spend a weekend outdoors without driving far. There is no fee for parking or camping, but *campers must register at headquarters and get a permit.* Campsites may be reserved as long as 60 days in advance (663-1092), and if you hope to use any during a holiday weekend you had better reserve them at least a month ahead of time. There's a one-night limit for each camp. This rule doesn't inflict any great hardship, since you can easily hike from one camp to another during the day.

In some parts of the backcountry the water is not potable. On day hikes, carry a canteen; on camping trips, check with headquarters in advance.

All the camps contain toilets, picnic tables, grills and hitchrails.

Because the peninsula is subject to frequent and unpredictable fogs, it's wise to take along some kind of cover for the night —if not a tent, at least a tarp.

The camps and some of the trails leading to them are described in subsequent pages. Incidentally, you don't have to backpack to visit these camps: each is close enough to some trailhead so that you can make it the destination for a picnic lunch on a one-day hike.

## Hostel

Point Reyes Hostel near Limantour Road is operated by the Golden Gate Council of American Youth Hostels, Inc. It is open every day of the year; check-in time is 4:30–9 p.m. Customs follow those of the International Youth Hostel Association (no pets, no alcohol, no smoking; curfew at 11 p.m.). Reservations are advised for groups larger than five.

Point Reyes Hostel, Box 247
Point Reyes Station, CA 94956
phone: 669-7414

For up-to-date information on fees, call the above number, or the San Francisco number of AYH Golden Gate Council: 771-4646 (10 a.m.–3 p.m. Monday through Saturday.)

## Swimming

The best swimming in the area is at Tomales Bay State Park (see pp. 68–73).

It is possible to swim at Drakes and Limantour beaches, though neither has lifeguard service—and the water at both is cold. Drakes has a bathhouse.

The powerful surf and unpredictable undertow make the ocean beaches much too dangerous for wading or swimming.

## Horses

Horses are permitted on many of the park trails; ask at headquarters. You can rent them at Bear Valley Stables (phone 663-1570) and at Five Brooks Stables (663-8287).

## Educational Programs

The rangers offer a variety of nature walks and other programs; inquire at the visitor centers.

The Coastal Parks Association in cooperation with the National Seashore sponsors programs of the Point Reyes Field Seminar, for some of which Dominican College offers credit. They cover a wide variety of subjects in natural history, education and the arts. Phone 663-1200.

The Point Reyes-Clem Miller Environmental Education Center offers summer camp for children (phone 663-1200).

The following organizations conduct hikes and field trips in the National Seashore:

Golden Gate Audubon Society
1550 Shattuck Avenue, #204
Berkeley, CA 94709
phone: 843-2222

Marin Audubon Society
Box 599
Mill Valley, CA 94942

California Native Plant Society
2380 Ellsworth Street, Suite D
Berkeley, CA 94704
phone: 841-5575

Sierra Club, San Francisco Bay Chapter
6014 College Avenue
Oakland, CA 94618
phone: 658-7470

Sierra Club, Marin Group
P.O. Box 5042
Mill Valley, CA 94942

Swimmers and waders take advantage of the warm water at Tomales Bay State Park

The blacksmith at the Morgan Horse Ranch demonstrates his ancient craft

Equestrians near the Morgan Horse Ranch in Bear Valley

25

# REGULATIONS

## Dogs

Proposals for governing dogs in the park have produced more intense and emotional testimony at Citizens' Advisory Commission meetings than almost any other subject except transportation. In the same way that many automobile owners feel, "I want to drive, but everyone else should take the bus," many dog owners feel, "*My* dog is well trained and always under control, so it should be allowed to go to the park with me, even if other people's dogs misbehave." The facts remain, however, that most dogs if allowed to run free just naturally chase deer and other wildlife, and some of them harass equestrians, hikers and bicyclists. And anyone who has hiked very long in the Bay Area knows that many dog owners simply ignore leash regulations. Therefore the National Seashore has adopted the following rules:

No dogs are allowed on trails, in campgrounds or on Drakes Beach, McClures Beach, or Limantour Beach west of the parking lot.

Dogs *on leash* are allowed on the following beaches: Kehoe, Abbotts Lagoon, Point Reyes North and South, Palomarin, and Limantour east of the parking lot.

## Bicycles

The use of bicycles or any other mechanical means of transit is prohibited in the wilderness area of the park. For more information on this subject, see the Supplement at the back of this book.

## Fires

Wood fires are prohibited in campgrounds. Use only charcoal, gas stoves or canned heat. Driftwood fires are permitted only on sandy beaches.

## Other Regulations

No fireworks, firearms or weapons of any kind are permitted.

Motorcycles are not permitted on trails.

## Observe warning signs on cliffs and beaches

It might seem unnecessary to belabor this point, yet two adult males were drowned at McClures Beach within two weeks during the spring of 1980, apparently because they ignored prominent signs warning of danger. The most hazardous activities are:

Wading or swimming in the treacherous surf of the ocean beaches;

Climbing on the cliffs above the ocean;

Getting trapped on a pocket beach by incoming tide. If you plan to beachcomb, check the tide tables in advance.

Great white sharks frequent the waters off Tomales Point. Although so far there have been no recorded shark-caused fatalities in the National Seashore, there have been several attacks on skin divers in the McClures Beach-Tomales Point area.

# MAPS

Headquarters issues some excellent maps containing much useful information. Other maps available at headquarters and at map stores in the Bay Area:

Molenaar, Dee, *Pictorial Landform Map: Point Reyes National Seashore and the San Andreas Fault.* Berkeley: Wilderness Press, 1982. Contains information about trails and facilities.

*Erickson's Map of Point Reyes National Seashore and Tomales Bay & Taylor State Parks...*

The US Geological Survey issues the most detailed and authoritative maps. They are available at map stores and at the USGS office at 555 Battery Street, San Francisco, and the USGS Western Regional Headquarters at 345 Middlefield Road, Menlo Park. "Point Reyes National Seashore and Vicinity" (scale 1:48,000) covers the whole peninsula and much of West Marin. "Point Reyes Quadrangle" (scale 1:62,500) covers most of the peninsula and is small enough to fold into a pocket. The five 7.5 minute topographic maps (scale 1:24,000) covering the National Seashore are: Tomales, Drakes Bay, Inverness, Double Point and Bolinas.

Many of the trails in the Seashore are old ranch roads that the park service has designated as official trails by mapping and signing them. There are a great many more old roads and trails that are not signed or officially maintained and that are not on any of the maps. Energetic and intrepid hikers can explore these at their leisure. If you know how to use a compass and the topographic maps, you will probably not get lost. A greater danger is poison oak, which abounds on some of the unmaintained trails.

## Point Reyes Station

This town was a stop on the North Pacific Coast Railroad from 1875 until the trains stopped running in 1933. The former depot is now the post office. Perhaps the town's greatest claim to fame nowadays is its Pulitzer Prize-winning weekly, the *Point Reyes Light*. (The *Light* won the award as a result of its investigatory reporting on neighboring Synanon Foundation.) Aficionados of offbeat journalism particularly relish the deadpan "Sheriff's Calls" that appear in each issue and illuminate life in West Marin. For example:

STINSON BEACH — Deputies responded to a report of a family fight in an apartment complex. When officers located the suspects, the suspects said they had merely been cleaning catfish and were unaware they were making noise. Deputies advised them to "chop quieter" if they were going to clean more catfish.

BOLINAS—Several drivers reported a skeleton jumping out in front of cars being driven around the lagoon. After officers checked the road they checked the cemetery and reported there was no evidence of a missing skeleton.

POINT REYES STATION—After overhearing an officer complain to another deputy that people only call the sheriff's office to inform him of bad news, a woman phoned the substation to report she had had "a nice day."

INVERNESS—A man advised deputies someone had unsuccessfully tried to break into his house. He realized burglary had been attempted when he found a note of apology wedged in the door from the would-be burglar.

# NEARBY TOWNS

Point Reyes Station contains restaurants, bars, grocery stores, a hardware store, a gas station and a branch of Bank of America.

## Olema

This town was once the metropolis of West Marin, until the North Pacific Coast Railroad bypassed it in 1875. Now Olema, at the crossroads of Drake Highway and Highway 1 near the main gateway to the park, contains a small grocery store and a restaurant with bar, Jerry's Farm House. The century-old Olema Inn (phone 663-8441) has been lovingly restored and now offers lunch, cocktails, dinner and Sunday brunch. It also has a few rooms for bed-and-breakfast.

## Inverness

When you drive to the western beaches of the National Seashore, you will pass through Inverness, founded as a resort town in the hope of restoring the Shafter family fortunes (see p. 18). The Shafter forebears were Scottish; hence the name of the town and streets such as Argyle and Cameron. Inverness contains motels, several restaurants and bed-and-breakfast houses, a grocery store, and a gas station.

## Bolinas

The citizens of Bolinas would prefer that no one know where it is.

**The outskirts of Inverness: buildings on Tomales Bay**

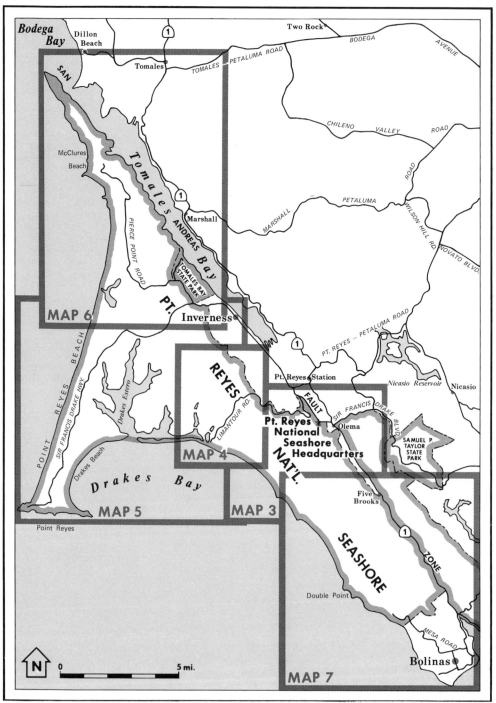

TOWNS NEAR THE NATIONAL SEASHORE
MAP 2

LEGEND:

——— Roads
- - - - Trail
▬▬▬ Park Bdy.
⊙ Campground

Misdirecting tourists, ripping out road signs, setting up blockades, trashing travel writers' cars, smashing realtors' windows, water-ballooning Winnebagos, stealing toilet paper rolls from public restrooms, erecting notices that their town is closed—these are just some of the many ways residents of West Marin's largest settlement have been trying to turn their home town into California's first unlisted community.
—Roger Rapoport, *San Francisco Chronicle*, March 17, 1978

As a result of these actions and attitudes, Bolinas has replaced Chico as a target for columnist Herb Caen's jibes: he called it "elitist, snobbish, ingrown, unfriendly and not the world's greatest place for food."

The fact remains that to reach the Palomarin trailhead of the National Seashore, you have to skirt Bolinas. If you decide to visit the business district of this misanthropic community (which contains restaurants, bars, a motel and a gas station), don't tell them I sent you.

### Recommended reading

Arrigoni, Patricia, *Making the Most of Marin*. Novato: Presidio Press, 1981.

---

## NOTE:

All telephone numbers in this book have area code 415 unless otherwise indicated.

The National Park Service is converting to the metric system by preferring kilometers in its trail signs and putting mileages in parentheses. I have followed this practice in giving trail distances. However, most of our automobiles do not yet have odometers that follow the metric system, so I have used only mileages in giving driving distances.

If you are checking the tide tables in a San Francisco newspaper, bear in mind that high tide at Point Reyes is about an hour earlier than at the Golden Gate.

The place names in this book conform to United State Geological Survey usage where sources differ. Hence, for example, this book has *Drakes Bay* (no apostrophe) and *Mt. Wittenberg* (not Wittenburg, as it appears on some publications of the California Division of Mines and Geology).

---

## MAP 2a
### BEAR VALLEY HEADQUARTERS AREA

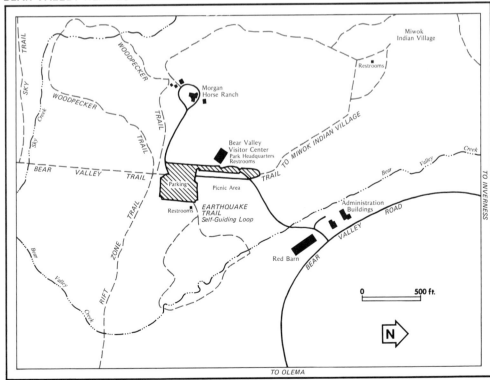

# THE TRAILS

## NATIONAL SEASHORE HEADQUARTERS

The Bear Valley visitor center opened in November 1983. It was financed with $1.4 million in private grants from the William Field Fund and the Buck Fund (via the San Francisco Foundation). The architects, Bull, Field, Volkmann & Stockwell, designed a 6800-square-foot barnlike structure intended to fit well into the surrounding pastoral landscape. It contains an auditorium, a library, office space and an extensive and fascinating exhibit area.

The visitor center should be your first stop in the park. Here you can pick up free maps and information sheets, find out what nature programs and other activities are scheduled, and browse in the book store. (Visitor center open weekdays 9 a.m.–5 p.m., weekends 8 a.m.–5 p.m.; phone 663-1092; water, restrooms, phone.)

First-time visitors to the park, tourists with little time to spare, and families with small children may wish to spend their entire stay in the Bear Valley area, rambling the short trails described below. Eventually the park service may establish a food concession here, but at present visitors must bring food or pick it up at one of the nearby communities if they wish to picnic at tables on the pleasant grounds under majestic firs, oaks and bay trees.

## EARTHQUAKE TRAIL

As this book went to press, the former Earthquake Trail was being rerouted and a 0.6–mile paved, self-guiding nature trail had just been constructed that is *completely accessible by wheelchair*. Those on foot will appreciate this gentle trail, too, as it winds across Bear Valley Creek under willows and oak trees in the area along the San Andreas Fault Zone where the land shifted abruptly by as much as 16 feet during the big quake of 1906.

More ambitious hikers who are seeking the Rift Zone Trail (see p. 36) can look for the sign just south of the Bear Valley parking lot.

---

Beauty in landscape is intimately connected with earthquakes, past or present. If one demands high mountains near broad oceans, it seems that one must put up with earthquakes.

> —Perry Byerly, "History of Earthquakes in the San Francisco Bay Area," in *Geologic Guidebook of the San Francisco Bay Counties.*

# BEAR VALLEY AND GLEN CAMP

"How do we get to the San Andreas Fault?"

Plaques along the Earthquake Trail show how the ground shifted 20 feet in 1906

# KULE LOKLO,
# THE MIWOK VILLAGE

You can gain some idea of how the original inhabitants of Point Reyes lived by paying a visit to the village of Kule Loklo (the Coast Miwok words for Bear Valley) less than a half mile north of headquarters. The village started in 1976 as a cooperative Bicentennial venture among the National Park Service, the Miwok Archeological Preserve of Marin, and a local school district. Much of the work has been done by schoolchildren and volunteers.

On weekends at the village you may find rangers and archeologists making arrow-

MIWOK VILLAGE WORKDAY
Point Reyes National Seashore rangers will hold a work day at Kule Loklo Miwok Village at Bear Valley all day Saturday. Park visitors are always invited to help.

Project director Greg Gnesios said tule will be available for mat weaving and kotca (hut) covering, willow for frame construction, and lots of rocks for reworking the dance house walls. He noted among other spring house-cleaning activities will be refurbishing a shabby acorn granary with bulrushes.

An afternoon pick-me-up of acorn mush will be served.

*Point Reyes Light*, April 17, 1980

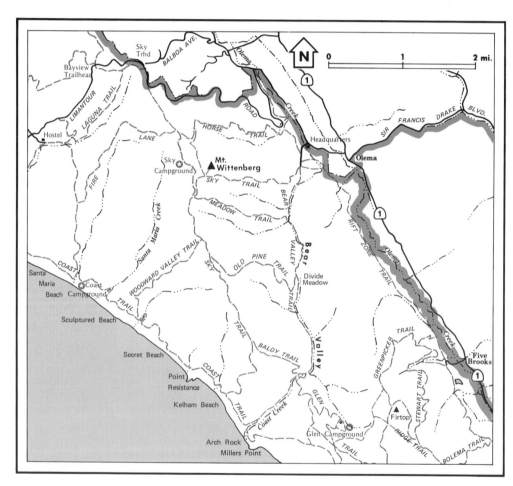

**BEAR VALLEY TRAILS**
MAP 3

LEGEND:
━━━━━ Roads
------ Trail
▰▰▰▰ Park Bdy.
⊙ Campground

heads out of obsidian from Sonoma County or weaving cooking baskets out of willow and sedge before an enthralled audience of young people.

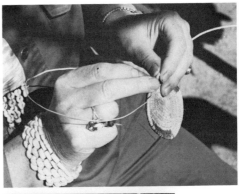

## WOODPECKER TRAIL AND THE MORGAN HORSE RANCH

The 1.1 km (.7 mile) Woodpecker Trail begins just north of the Bear Valley parking lot and trailhead, on the right, and runs gently uphill toward the forest. The self-guiding trail is marked by explanatory posts that point out the main kinds of trees and other natural features of the Point Reyes area, including a particular Douglas fir which has been much favored by California woodpeckers.

Still in the forest, the trail curves north and east around a small meadow. If you are lucky and quiet, you may see some white fallow deer browsing here. Now the trail comes out at a red barn/museum where you can study the fascinating history of the Morgan horse, the first truly American breed. All Morgans are descended from one superequine, a stallion who died in 1821 after distinguishing himself for strength, speed and endurance. After studying their background, you can watch the park's current herd of Morgans frisking about in their corral. The park service raises these horses to provide visitors—especially city children—a chance to experience first hand an important part of our country's heritage, and also to provide mounts for rangers at the Seashore and other national parks.

## BEAR VALLEY TRAIL

This is undoubtedly the most popular trail in the National Seashore—and with good reason. It's an easy, fairly level walk alongside murmuring streams, under towering trees and through a broad, peaceful meadow, eventually arriving at the sea. Don't expect solitude, however: this trail is generally thronged with hikers on weekends. The Bear Valley Trail has always been popular with bicyclists. However, its final ¾ mile is in the Seashore wilderness area, and therefore currently off limits to bikes, pending further clarification of NPS policy.

The whole distance is 7 km (4.4 miles). There is no drinking water anywhere along the route. There are toilets at Divide Meadow, roughly the midpoint.

The trailhead is just south of the parking lot. As you start out on the trail, you will be

A volunteer demonstrates traditional basket making at the Miwok Village, Kule Loklo

Young visitors admire the handsome Morgan horses in their corral near the Bear Valley trailhead

Rest stop at Divide Meadow on the Bear Valley Trail

The end of the Bear Valley Trail: Arch Rock Overlook

walking beside Bear Valley Creek. This stream runs north—the opposite direction from the stream you will hike along after passing the meadow. Odd drainage patterns are characteristic of the fault zone.

Hikers who have not visited Bear Valley since January 1982 will find that the trail is not always in the same relation to the creeks as formerly. The storms of that year did monumental damage to the trail, which had to be extensively rebuilt in places. The riprap along the streambanks appeared harsh and awkward at first, but nature has softened it in the intervening years.

In ¼ mile you pass the Sky Trail junction, marked by a gigantic bay tree with many trunks. Now you enter a forested area, with bay, Douglas fir, bishop pine, buckeye, hazel, elderberry and, along the stream, alder. In places the larger trees arch over the trail to form a leafy tunnel through which sunlight filters. Ferns abound on the mossy bands—five-finger and maidenhair, as well as the more common sword and bracken ferns. If you are hiking in spring, you will find buttercup, iris, miner's lettuce, bleeding heart, wild cucumber, blue forget-me-not, English daisy, and—if you look closely along the stream bank—wild ginger.

After 2.4 km (1.6 miles) of gentle ascent from the trailhead, you arrive at Divide Meadow (toilets, picnic tables). San Francisco's elite Pacific Union Club maintained its hunting lodge here from the 1890s until the Great Depression. Their quarry included bear and mountain lion, as well as deer.

Helen Bingham, who visited Point Reyes in 1906, described Bear Valley in her book *In Tamal Land*:

"One can drive through its cool depths on a finely graded road amid thousands of majestic trees, while here and there an open space reveals the sunlight and the blue sky overhead in contrast with the dim, uncertain light pervading its woodland stretches." She took a dim view of the hunt club, however: "The deep baying of hounds from its extensive kennels forms the only discordant note in the Valley, reminding one that even near to nature's heart man's inherent primitiveness asserts itself. If, when wandering in these woodland fastnesses, he (man) would hunt the wild creatures with a camera it would require greater patience, skill and acumen than making the ground wet with the blood of fawns and quail."

As we walk through the now-peaceful meadow, it is pleasant to observe that Miss Bingham's wish has been fulfilled.

After following the edge of the long meadow, the trail reenters forest. The

stream accompanying it now is Coast Creek, which flows into the ocean. The unusually large buckeyes along this part of the trail are magnificent in late spring, when their candles of pinkish-cream flowers are blooming.

Finally you come out on a meadow about 50 feet above the sea—an old marine terrace that has been raised sometime within the last 100,000 years. If the tide is low enough, you can descend a steep trail to the beach and a natural rock tunnel through which the creek flows. Or you can walk out Miller Point to look up and down the coast. A circular marker shows the points of the compass and the principal sights.

You can return to the trailhead the way you came, or if the day is still young and you don't mind a climb, you can use your trail map to work out an alternative route or a scenic detour.

**Returning toward the Bear Valley trailhead under arching bay trees**

# RIFT ZONE TRAIL

## How To Get There

The trail runs for almost 5 level miles between Bear Valley and Five Brooks.

BY BUS: If you come by bus, you necessarily start at Bear Valley and either walk roundtrip, or make a long loop by way of Firtop and/or Glen Camp, or cadge a ride back from the Five Brooks parking lot to the Bear Valley bus stop.

BY CAR: You can park at either Bear Valley or Five Brooks, 3½ miles south. If you want to walk the trail just one way, you can arrange a car shuttle, leaving one car in each parking lot. Since the route is virtually level, it doesn't much matter which direction you choose to walk in. I have arbitrarily written it up as starting from Bear Valley because that's where the bus stops.

Facilities: Water, restrooms and picnic tables at Bear Valley and Five Brooks.

Heading toward the Olema Valley
on the Rift Zone Trail

## Regulations:

The trail crosses land belonging to the Vedanta Society, and hikers should observe their rules: open 8 a.m. until two hours before sunset; no wheeled vehicles, no hunting, no dogs or other pets, no fires or smoking, no camping or picnicking. There are many livestock gates along the route, which hikers should close after going through them.

The first time I tried this trail was at the end of a long, dry summer. Not only was the trail extremely dusty to begin with, but as we hiked north from Five Brooks we encountered over a hundred equestrians spread out along it, who—although friendly—could hardly avoid stirring up even more dust. I mentally wrote this trail off as suitable mainly for horsepersons, and repaired to Jerry's Farm House in Olema for a beer.

A year and a half later, some visitors from the East Coast expressed such eagerness to hike along the San Andreas Fault Zone that I agreed to accompany them from Bear Valley to Five Brooks. It was a warm day in early April, and the countryside still sported the vivid early-Technicolor green that exhilarates inhabitants of northern California for about three weeks of every year. Over the entire 5 miles we encountered only three other hikers and one equestrian. The Easterners were so entranced by the idyllic gorgeousness of this trail that they begged me never to publicize it. (But duty prevails.)

The Rift Zone Trails begins just south of the Bear Valley parking lot. It crosses Bear Valley Creek, then ascends a knoll under bay trees and coast live oaks. You go through a self-closing livestock gate and traverse a meadow, heading toward the line of eucalyptus and Monterey cypress that marks the road to the Vedanta Society Retreat. Two gates permit hikers to cross this road. In the next 3 miles you will be hiking on Vedanta Society land.

The Vedanta Society is a religious organization whose beliefs are basically East Indian in origin. Its main northern California headquarters is at 2323 Vallejo Street, San Francisco 94123 (phone 922-2323). Its Olema Retreat is designed to "provide opportunity to spiritual seekers of all faiths to meditate and study in a secluded area of meadows and forests away from the disturbances of urban life." Originally this land belonged to Judge James McMillan Shafter and after him his son Payne. The Vedanta Society purchased it in 1946. According to a long-standing agreement with the Department of the Interior, the society may continue to maintain its 2000-plus acres as a religious retreat, with the stipulation that if it ever desires to sell any of its land the National Seashore will have the first option to buy it.

Once past the Vedanta Society's gate you make your way across a large field, heading for the corral at the south end. Soon the old Shafter mansion "The Oaks" comes into view at the end of the tree-lined driveway. This magnificent house, built in 1869, is now headquarters for the Vedanta Society Retreat. A number of devotees live here permanently and raise fruit, vegetables and dairy products; hence the barn and other outbuildings.

Going counterclockwise around the corral, you turn left on a graveled road as per the trail sign. The next 2 miles are on this road, which runs south through countryside of great beauty and variety. Cool ferny forests alternate with tranquil meadows and mysterious marshes. Occasional fallen bay trees form leafy arches over the trail. You are paralleling Highway 1 (as well as Olema Creek and the San Andreas Fault Zone) but are just far enough away from it not to hear auto noises.

Shortly after leaving Vedanta property you descend some "stairs" in the trail suitable for equestrians as well as hikers. You cross a creek and pass a trail on the right that leads to Firtop. (The sign *Amanda Way* along this section of trail is not a Vedantic inscription but refers to a member of the Stewart family, who own a nearby ranch.)

After walking past another marsh, you ford another creek and arrive at a horse camp. Walk across its clearing heading for the house with a picket fence on the south side. You go briefly back into forest and soon emerge on the main road headed for the Five Brooks parking lot. Along the way you get a good view of Bolinas Ridge to the east.

From the Rift Zone Trail hikers can get a glimpse of the Vedanta Society Retreat, formerly James M. Shafter's mansion "The Oaks"

Bay trees form a virtual roof above the Rift Zone Trail on the Vedanta Society's land

# GLEN CAMP

## Facilities:
Water, but during some seasons it is not potable—find out from headquarters in advance; toilets, picnic tables, grills, hitchrail.

## Regulations:
No dogs, no open fires. (It is not a regulation, but insect repellent is advisable in warm weather.)

The trail to Glen Camp passes under majestic old Douglas firs

Campsites are spread out around the glen; some are sheltered by trees

In some respects Glen Camp is the most attractive of the backpacking camps in the National Seashore. True, it lacks the views one gets at Sky Camp, and it lacks the beaches one finds at Wildcat and Coast camps. But its campsites are more widely dispersed, and some are sheltered under towering trees, so that a camper gets a little more feeling of remoteness.

A glance at the map reveals that Glen Camp can be approached from either Bear Valley trailhead or Five Brooks trailhead. Although Five Brooks is closer to the camp as the crow flies, the route from Bear Valley is leveller. Take the Bear Valley Trail 4.8 km (3 miles) to the clearly marked turnoff to Glen Camp on the left. (In spring, a purple nightshade blooms on your right just before the turnoff.) The Glen Camp Trail (more of a fire road at this point) leads uphill and through a meadow, offering a glimpse of the ocean. Now the trail turns east and becomes a tree-shaded path skirting a canyon. You walk through coffeeberry and lots of blackberry, and at one point cross a stream. Following the signs to Glen Camp, you make a short descent past a marshy pond and then a brief climb into the protected glade around which the campsites are scattered.

The quickest, easiest way to return is the way you came. However, if you've camped overnight, and lightened your pack by eating and drinking part of the contents, you may be game for a somewhat more ambitious hike. A look at the map reveals several possibilities. For example, you can go back to the Bear Valley Trail, cross it, and return to the trailhead via Baldy and Sky trails and Mt. Wittenberg (about 9.6 km, or 6 miles, including an elevation gain of over 1300 feet). Or you can take one of the trails to Five Brooks and then hike the 8 km (5 mile) Rift Zone Trail back to headquarters—or hitchhike back with a hiker who has parked at Five Brooks.

Or you can wander around the Highland Loop and take the Coast Trail back to Bear Valley. This route will take you through some of the wildest and least traveled areas of the park. Parts of the Coast Trail south of Bear Valley are steep, rocky and rugged. Clem Miller, the late Congressman who was probably more responsible than any other one person for establishing the National Seashore, is buried under a simple stone a short distance from the Coast Trail, on a bluff overlooking the ocean above the point that bears his name.

## How To Get There
Begin at Bear Valley trailhead.

## Facilities:
Water, toilets, picnic tables, grills, hitchrail at Sky Camp.

## Regulations:
No dogs, no open fires.

Mt. Wittenberg, at 1407 feet, is the highest point in the National Seashore and offers a grand view over the surrounding country. On its western flank is Sky Camp, one of four backpacking camps in the park, and the one closest to headquarters. Sky Camp is short on privacy, since most of the campsites are on open hillside. It is long on views, however, and is very popular.

Mt. Wittenberg is an excellent destination for a day hike, planning lunch for either the summit or Sky Camp. With the aid of your trail map, you can choose among several possible routes of varying degrees of steepness and devise a loop trip to suit your mood and the weather.

## SKY TRAIL

This is the most direct hiking route to Sky Camp—only 4 km (2.5 miles)—but it is also the steepest. Novice backpackers and leisurely picnickers may prefer one of the gentler routes.

Start on the Bear Valley Trail, and in ¼ mile turn right on clearly marked Sky Trail at the great multiple-trunked bay tree. The trail ascends under hazel, tanbark oak and Douglas fir; a profusion of sword ferns carpets the ground. About halfway up the mountain you come to a near-level clearing somewhat larger than a football field where you can catch your breath. In fall you can search for huckleberries in the lush growth bordering the clearing.

The trail now continues up an open slope dotted with firs, then goes steeply through forest again and finally emerges on a hillside not far from the top of the mountain. A short trail leads to the summit. From here you have a 360-degree view of the entire Point Reyes peninsula and the esteros, Tomales Bay, Black Mountain (also known as Elephant Mtn.) behind Point Reyes Station, the lush Olema Valley and Bolinas Ridge; and in clear weather Mts. St. Helena, Diablo and Tamalpais.

From the summit you descend south to rejoin the Sky Trail. Here you can turn right to reach Sky Camp, or turn left to take one of

Before the final ascent of Mt. Wittenberg, the Sky Trail levels off in a long meadow

the trails leading back to Bear Valley or the coast.

## MEADOW TRAIL

This route offers hikers and backpackers a more gradual ascent to Sky Camp than the Sky Trail. Take the Bear Valley Trail past the Sky Trail junction and turn right on the Meadow Trail, 1 km (.6 mile) from the trailhead. The trail ascends through pungent bay, tall Douglas fir, dense sword fern and bushy huckleberry. On one cool November day on which I hiked here, the forest silence was broken only by the songs of a couple of varied thrushes (*Ixoreus naevius*). It was the first clear day after a week of rain, and I found an incredibly lush and varied growth of mushrooms.

The trail soon reaches the long meadow of its name. On that visit, I encountered in the very center of the long meadow a solitary young man in the half-lotus position playing a flute. Perhaps he was trying to charm some of the animals out of the ground. To judge from the number of burrows, the meadow must support a considerable subterranean population of rabbits, weasels, badgers or foxes. If there are no flute players, and you come by yourself or in a small, quiet group, you have an excellent chance of seeing deer.

From the meadow, the trail reenters forest and continues to ascend gently, occasionally overlooking a deep, wooded canyon. The trees here are so tall that as you walk beneath them you can hear the wind soughing in their tops, sounding like a distant waterfall, but you cannot feel it. Soon you reach the Sky Trail junction, and from here it's only a level half mile straight ahead to the camp. If the day is clear, you will have views of Limantour Spit and Drakes Bay as you contour along the slope of Mt. Wittenberg.

## HORSE TRAIL

Hikers seldom use this trail, perhaps because they figure it's the province of horses; but if you try it on a weekday you probably won't run into many equestrians. It provides a different and pleasant way to reach Sky Camp. (It can, however, get muddy in places during the rainy season; and slogging through mud that has just been trodden by horses will test the mettle—and the boots—of even the most dedicated hiker.)

From the parking lot, head toward the Miwok Village. The Horse Trail branches off at a sign before you reach the village and curves around it, under firs and bay trees. In a half mile a trail to the stables branches off right. The Horse Trail turns left and runs above and generally parallel to Limantour Road. It ascends gradually under bay and oak trees, crossing a creek and then following it for a while. An occasional break in the forest offers a view of Mt. Wittenberg. After a little over 3 km (2 miles) the trail comes out in the open as you crest Inverness Ridge, and soon you have your choice of junctions: you can climb Mt. Wittenberg, or go a little farther and turn left on the Sky Trail to Sky Camp, or go a little farther still and turn right on the Fire Lane Trail.

**Lunch on the west side of Mt. Wittenberg**

Several varieties of deadly Amanita mushrooms grow near the trails on Mt. Wittenberg

Approaching Sky Camp from the summit of Mt. Wittenberg; fog veils Drakes Bay in the distance

# TRAILS FROM SKY CAMP TO BEAR VALLEY AND TO THE COAST

Douglas firs tower a hundred feet above Sky Trail

With the aid of your trusty trail map you can work out several attractive loops.

## OLD PINE TRAIL

An easy and beautiful route back to Bear Valley is by the Old Pine Trail. From Sky Camp take the Sky Trail south, passing the Meadow Trail junction at 1 km (.6 mile). Continue on the Sky Trail under majestic, moss-covered firs that reach straight above you for a hundred feet or more. Some have leather fern growing from their trunks and branches, and elderberry, blackberry, huckleberry and salal provide a green undergrowth. This dense forest conveys a sense of peace—and yet of mystery, too.

You pass the Woodward Valley Trail going off to the right in a small glade, and after a short km (½ mile) turn left on Old Pine Trail. It descends for 1½ km to Divide Meadow, still mainly under large firs. It gets its name, however, from a small grove of bishop pine trees in the forest of Douglas firs. From Divide Meadow it's 2.4 km (1.6 miles) north (left) on Bear Valley Trail back to the trailhead.

The Old Pine Trail was closed for many months because of storm damage during the rough winters of 1982 and 1983. The trail was reopened late in 1984, but remnants of the storm are still very evident in the form of down trees—some of which fell athwart the trail and had to be sawed through by the trail crew.

## WOODWARD VALLEY TRAIL

This varied trail alternates dense forest with open greensward, and features occasional sudden and spectacular views over Drakes Bay and the ocean. Because of the views and the occasional steep stretches, I prefer to hike this trail heading west—that is to say, descending.

The Woodward Valley Trail branches off from the Sky Trail 2.2 km (1.4 miles) from Sky Camp at a glade. The trail enters forest, then passes through a long, enchanted meadow fringed with firs. It is tempting just to throw down one's knapsack and spend the day here, snoozing and hoping for a visit from the white deer—or even a unicorn.

From the meadow you continue back into the forest, then soon emerge into the open and a view of Limantour; if the weather is clear enough, the Farallon Islands are visible on the horizon 20 miles out to sea. From here on, the trail goes in and out of woods, generally descending—at times steeply.

Soon the panorama includes the whole of Drakes Bay from Double Point to Point Reyes.

At 2.7 km (1.7 miles) from the Sky Trail junction, the Woodward Valley Trail joins the Coast Trail just above Sculptured Beach (see p. 45). You can visit the beach and then proceed south to Bear Valley or north to Coast Camp and Limantour.

## SKY AND BALDY TRAILS

The Sky Trail south from its junction with the Meadow Trail and past the Woodward Valley and Old Pine Trail junctions runs through the dense fir forest of Inverness Ridge. If you continue south on the Sky

Trail, after another mile of forest you will come out in the open facing Baldy, a bare knob 1034 feet high. A fork here offers two choices: The Baldy Trail on the left leads 1.6 km (1 mile) down to the Bear Valley Trail at its intersection with the Glen Camp Trail; from here it's about 5 km (3 miles) back to the Bear Valley Trailhead. Or you can continue on the Sky Trail, overlooking Drakes Bay and the ocean; the trail soon begins a descent that becomes fairly steep toward its end, at the junction with the Coast Trail just south of Kelham Beach.

**Mt. Wittenberg seen from the Old Pine Trail**

43

## COAST CAMP

### Facilities:
Water, toilets, picnic tables, grills, hitchrail.

### Regulations:
No dogs, no open fires.

Coast Camp, which is just a few hundred feet from attractive Santa Maria Beach, is protected by a sandy ridge from ocean winds. The campsites, spread out on a treeless plain, don't offer much privacy, but this consideration seems not to bother the young and the gregarious who flock to it on weekends.

Actually, the easiest, shortest way to get to Coast Camp is to drive to the Limantour Spit parking lot and walk 2½ km (1½ miles) southeast on the beach. This is an excellent idea for a leisurely afternoon picnic, but not a very enterprising backpack trip for a weekend.

Whichever route you choose to Coast Camp, check a tide table or the newspaper before setting out, so you'll know when you can visit nearby Sculptured Beach, which is accessible only at low tide.

## COAST TRAIL NORTH

The 12.8 km (8 mile) route from headquarters along the Bear Valley Trail and north on the Coast Trail is mostly level and very scenic.

Take the Bear Valley Trail (see p. 33) for 6.4 km (4 miles) and turn right on the Coast Trail. This old farm road runs along an ancient marine terrace now raised a couple of hundred feet above the ocean. If the day is clear, you can see the Farallon Islands and Point Reyes as you walk along it.

About a mile from Bear Valley Trail is a junction with the access trail to Kelham Beach, which has a picnic table under a giant eucalyptus. The road continues along the headlands for about 3 km (2 miles). Shortly past a small gulch, Woodward Valley Trail goes off to the right and the trail to Sculptured Beach to the left. If the tide is low enough you can visit this fascinating beach by making a short descent. The fantastically eroded, layered rocks offer marvelous opportunities for studying sea anemones and other tidepool life. The ochre cliffs, also obviously in the process of eroding, in places form bizarrely contoured canyons. As these cliffs are much too steep to climb, be sure to keep an eye on the tide.

When the tide is *really* low, you can visit

Some people look . . .

. . . others listen

Pelicans, cormorants and seagulls perch on a seastack off the Coast Trail

Secret Beach, south of Sculptured Beach.

At low tide you can proceed to Coast Camp on the beach—the most direct route. Or you can climb back up to the Coast Trail, which makes a V inland to cross Santa Maria Creek under willows and alders, then passes under a jutting rock formation and arrives at the camp.

From the camp you can proceed northwest to Limantour by walking about 2½ km (1½ miles) on the beach. Or you can continue northwest on the Coast Trail, passing the Fire Lane Trail on your right. Coast Trail proper ends at the Point Reyes Hostel, 4 km (2½ miles) from Coast Camp. To reach Limantour instead, you can leave the Coast Trail to skirt the marsh and hike along the dunes.

## FROM SKY CAMP TO COAST CAMP

Because Sky Camp is 800 feet higher than Coast Camp, most hikers and backpackers would probably prefer to take them in this order. There are two routes between the camps. The route of choice used to be the Beatty Trail, but it was closed because of storm damage in 1982 and is no longer on the park maps. A route runing parallel to it, the Fire Lane Trail, begins a short half mile north of Sky Camp and runs for just over 3 miles to Coast Camp. Along the way it offers sweeping views of the ocean.

Another possible route between Sky and Coast camps is by the Sky, Woodward Valley and Coast trails (see pp. 42-43).

Looking across Drakes Bay to Point Reyes Head from the Beatty Trail

## How To Get There

BY CAR: From headquarters, drive north a mile on Bear Valley Road, turn left on Limantour Road and follow it to the end.

## Facilities:
Water, toilets, phone.

## Regulations:
Dogs on leash are allowed on Limantour Beach east of the parking lot; dogs are not allowed at all on the west side, which is a Research Natural Area.

Estero de Limantour and its accompanying beach and sandspit are named for one of those outrageous characters who pop up from time to time in the annals of 19th century California. Jose Yves Limantour, a naturalized Mexican of French descent, loaded up the trading ship *Ayacucho* with luxury goods in 1841 and sailed from Mexico, aiming for San Francisco. Instead, he overshot the Golden Gate and ran aground on this sandspit. (This was the second shipwreck in Drakes Bay; the first was Cermeno's in 1595. See p. 18). Leaving his cargo on the beach, Limantour headed for San Francisco, toward which a friendly Indian had pointed the way. In the City he hired a ship's captain to recover the cargo, but

A western grebe enjoys the protected Limantour Natural Area

A busy Sunday afternoon at Limantour Beach

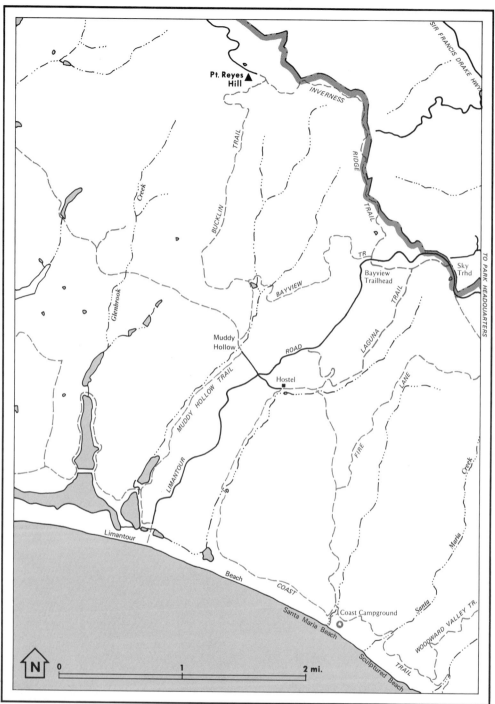

**THE LIMANTOUR AREA**
MAP 4

**LEGEND:**

———— Roads
– – – – Trail
━━━ Park Bdy.
⊙ Campground

48

gave him such poor directions that the man ended up instead in Bolinas Lagoon. Next, Limantour himself led an overland party to fetch the treasure, but got lost. Finally John Reed, the first Mexican land grantee in Marin County, led Limantour to the goods.

In the 1850s Limantour claimed to have received from former governor Micheltorena grants of 600,000 acres, including half of San Francisco. Limantour pocketed between $250,000 and $500,000 from unsuspecting land buyers until 1858, when the Federal Government ruled that his documents were forgeries. By this time he had escaped to Mexico.

## THE ROAD TO LIMANTOUR

As we noted on page 20, the northern section of the Limantour Road was constructed in 1966, when the park planners were still thoroughly auto-oriented. Even then, environmentalists and downslope property owners objected to the construction of such a broad road on steep and unstable terrain so near the San Andreas Fault. The property owners filed suit to block its construction, but the suit was thrown out because—according to one of them—"the presiding federal judge was incapable of reading a map." During the storm of January 1982 slides occurred on the controversial new part of the road, and the Park Service closed the entire road to the public. Lack of funds prevented repair of the road for over a year, and in March 1983 another slide displaced a further 60-yard-long section of pavement.

For months afterwards extensive negotiations took place among the downslope property owners, the NPS, the Federal Highway Administration and representatives of Congresswoman Boxer. One West Marin resident, Elizabeth Whitney, suggested in the Bolinas *Coastal Post* a novel alternative to rebuilding the road:

> My proposal is to not repair the road, but to build a safe pedestrian walkway across the slide. This walkway could have interpretive signs describing the storm and giving information relevant to the geological process exposed in the slide. It would be the Flood Trail, complementing the Earthquake Trail. . . . As for access to the beach, the simple solution would be a pair of small shuttle vans on the other side of the slide to take people into the park, to the Youth Hostel, and to the beach on a frequent schedule.

The powers that be, however, decided not to adopt this innovative solution, and instead

**Beautiful Limantour Beach inspires euphoria in some visitors**

rebuilt the road, which reopened in the fall of 1984.

# LIMANTOUR BEACH AND MUDDY HOLLOW

It was the area above Limantour Beach that was scheduled for subdivision as Drakes Beach Estates in the 1950s. Early in 1961, George Dusheck reported in the San Francisco *News-Call-Bulletin*: "The stakes are up, with fluttering blue and red ribbons attached, on the half-acre homesites. Architects and engineers are at work on plans to dredge a small boat harbor, lay out a golf course, and erect a Carmel-type commercial development." This was one of the prospects that spurred conservationists and the National Park Service into action to establish the National Seashore. A few houses remain on the bluff above the beach; now they are residences of park personnel.

In some respects Limantour Beach is the most idyllic in the Seashore. The ponds and marshes of its Protected Natural Area are a virtual paradise for birders and students of nature. Beachcombers can frolic and wade along miles of clean white sand, enjoying on a clear day the view over Drakes Bay all the way from Double Point to Chimney Rock. Hikers can go south on the beach or over the bluffs to Coast Camp, and at low tide on to Sculptured Beach.

Another good hike of about four miles, or more if desired, is to Muddy Hollow. During the wet season it *is* muddy, so wear appropriate footgear. From the west end of the Limantour parking lot find the Bayview trailhead (sign). You walk along the edge of a marsh through coyote brush, and soon the sound of the waves behind you dims as you curve inland. You pass a causeway dividing a lagoon. Ducks frequent this lagoon, and in winter you may see some migrants from the north. Continuing past alders and willows, you proceed up a valley between mostly bare rolling hills, through a grove of alders and then one of pines. Some pampas grass adds an exotic touch. As I walked alone on this trail one fall day I encountered at least a dozen small rabbits which scampered into the brush at my approach.

After 3 km (1.9 miles) of level walking you reach the Muddy Hollow parking lot and trailhead (amply signed). Now several possibilities beckon:

You can head over toward the nearby cypress grove, picnic there, and return the way you came.

Setting off through alders
on the way to Muddy Hollow

"Can that be a Lapland longspur?"

You can walk over to Limantour Road, cross it, walk toward the hostel and thence down toward the beach and the parking lot.

You can continue on the Bayview Trail across a culvert to a junction where signs indicate the routes to Bayview (uphill 2 miles) and to Estero trailhead (6.6 miles) and proceed along either of them.

## OTHER TRAILS IN THE LIMANTOUR AREA

When the shuttle bus was running, it was possible to make all-downhill hikes from Bayview or Summit trailhead to Limantour and return by bus. Nowadays hikers who want to try these scenic downhill hikes can arrange a two-car shuttle.

## SKY TRAILHEAD TO LIMANTOUR VIA POINT REYES HOSTEL

For a mostly downhill scenic hike, leave one car at Limantour and take another to the parking lot at Sky (formerly Summit) trailhead. Look for the Bayview Trail just south of the entrance to the parking lot. This trail runs parallel to the road, mostly level, for .7 miles through blackberry, cow parsnip and coyote brush, under Douglas firs, coast live oaks and occasional bishop pines. Where the Bayview Trail turns right at a signed junction, continue on the Laguna Trail. After a brief uphill stretch you look over a ridge toward the ocean (or a sea of fog). The trail —much of which is actually the remains of an old road—then descends, at times fairly steeply, and finally levels off at the Clem Miller Environmental Center (water, restrooms). The park service hopes to be able to raise private funds to replace the aging quonset hut that functions as a classroom. A modern development is the solar-heated shower facility.

A possible side trip here is the Hidden Valley Trail, a .6-mile loop constructed by the Stuart Hall for Boys (a private school in San Francisco) as part of the park's Adopt-a-Trail program. This shady, leafy trail offers a nice contrast to the more open roads that constitute the rest of this route.

Now take the paved road past the quonset hut, turn left, and after about a hundred feet go through a gate, passing on the left a road leading to a park residence. A little farther along the road is the Point Reyes Hostel (open 4:30-9 p.m.; phone 669-7414). At a fork in the road just beyond the hostel, bear left, as per the sign COAST TRAIL. You walk along a creek bordered with willows and alders, between two rows of low, scrub-covered hills. After about a mile on this road, follow an arrow sign left and cross the creek on a bridge. Soon the road curves right, toward the ocean, and passes a marsh full of cattails. At last the ocean comes into view beyond grass-covered dunes. The road skirts a lagoon that is usually full of birdlife.

Now you can choose whether to stay on the road and proceed southeast a mile to Coast Camp, or to head over the dunes toward the beach and northwest to the Limantour parking lot.

A modern Audubon painting the shorebirds of Limantour Estero

## MT. VISION AND
## POINT REYES HILL

### How To Get There

BY CAR: From Bear Valley headquarters take Bear Valley Road north, bear left on Sir Francis Drake Highway and continue on Drake through Inverness to the Pierce Point Road junction (7½ miles from headquarters). Bear left to stay on Drake. The Mt. Vision turnoff is a mile beyond the junction. The 3-mile-long road up the mountain is narrow, twisting and potholed—not suitable for trailers.

### Facilities:

None except parking.

### Regulations:

No dogs.

Point Reyes Hill at 1336 feet and Mt. Vision at 1282 feet are the second and third highest places in the National Seashore, ranking only after Mt. Wittenberg (1407 feet). At the Mt. Vision parking lot, which overlooks a pond, a sign indicates the short trail to the summit. From the summit, weather permitting, you can have a grand view over the whole peninsula and see Mts. St. Helena, Diablo and Tamalpais—our constant landmarks from the high parts of the National Seashore. In spring this short walk delights one with a profusion of wildflowers: not only the ubiquitous poppy and lupine, but also seaside daisy, baby blue eyes, harvest brodiaea, wild hollyhock, paintbrush, yarrow and navarretia, popularly called skunkweed because of its odor.

From the Mt. Vision parking lot you can drive another .6 mile to the Point Reyes Hill parking lot and walk up the hill on a paved road. Or you can walk southeast from Mt. Vision's summit to Point Reyes Hill on the remains of an old road. This route has been getting more and more overgrown, not only with coyote brush but also with *poison oak*, so caution is advisable. Four acres at the top of Point Reyes Hill are leased to the Federal Aviation Administration to house a directional signal that guides planes to the San Francisco airport.

**Are these "the cliffs of Nova Albion"?**

# ALONG
# SIR FRANCIS DRAKE
# HIGHWAY

### ESTERO TRAIL

### How to get there

BY CAR: The road leading to the trailhead branches left from Drake Highway .8 mile west of the road to Mt. Vision.

### Facilities:

Toilets at trailhead; no water along the route.

The Estero Trail leads for 7.4 km (4.6 miles) over open, gently rolling downs along the shore of Home Bay to Drakes Estero. The virtually treeless route does not provide the diversity of terrain and vegetation that one finds on hikes in the more southerly portion of the Seashore. On the other hand, it offers a grand opportunity to see wildlife. The mudflats bordering Drakes Estero are a feeding ground for a great number of shore

Looking toward Mt. Wittenberg from the bushy trail near the summit of Mt. Vision

and water birds, and on the way there you will also see land birds. You will almost certainly see cattle—since this area is still devoted to daily farming—and probably deer, and perhaps harbor seals.

Begin by going through a hiker's stile and gently uphill. Looking back, you can see Inverness Ridge, with Mt. Vision, Point Reyes Hill and Mt. Wittenberg silhouetted. In the near distance is Home Ranch. Cresting the low hill you overlook a marsh. On one hike here with an Audubon group we discovered a large herd of mixed species of deer on the hillside above the marsh: native black-tailed, spotted axis and white-to-buff fallow. The fallow bucks sported large antlers, giving them an elklike appearance.

The trail descends past an old cypress and a former Christmas tree farm, which has been suggested as a possible site for an overnight camp. You cross a causeway over an inlet of Home Bay. A sign advises: *Don't touch seal pups—mother will abandon any pups touched*. I have never seen seal pups here, but I have seen many egrets.

The trail gradually ascends again to overlook the mudflats of Home Bay, Drakes Estero, and the Johnson Oyster Company's beds (see p. 55). As you walk above the shore you might try to imagine the lively scenes here a hundred years ago, when the channel was navigable by schooner. A

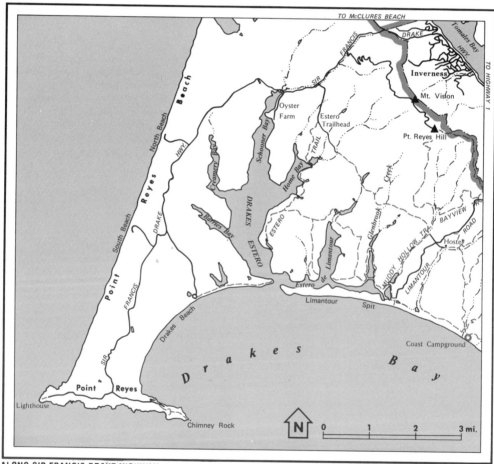

ALONG SIR FRANCIS DRAKE HIGHWAY

MAP 5

LEGEND:

━━━━━ Roads
─────── Trail
▄▄▄▄▄ Park Bdy.
◘ Campground

200-foot-long pier extended into Schooner Bay. Here the ships brought in feed and grain and picked up the very best butter, bound for the City. They also picked up live hogs. Historian Jack Mason noted, "If one fell in the water, it was a battle recovering him: Point Reyes hogs were, as we know, ferocious." Even larger schooners brought redwood lumber in from Santa Cruz.

You continue above the shore of Home Bay and then of Drakes Estero, crossing two more causeways. Along the way you may see great blue herons, godwits, willets, canvasbacks, buffleheads, ruddy ducks and American widgeons, depending on the season and your luck, After the third causeway a sign indicates the trail to Muddy Hollow, about 6½ km (4 miles) away. Anyone who wants a long ramble over open country could arrange a car-shuttle between the Estero and Muddy Hollow trailheads.

The trail descends to its final causeway near the sandy mouth of the estero. You can wander around the shore and look for harbor seals, which frequent the estero's sandspits.

# JOHNSON'S OYSTER FARM

**Address:**   P.O. Box 68
                    Inverness, CA 94937

**Phone:**   669-1149

**Hours:**   weekdays 8 a.m.-4:30 p.m.,
                 weekends 9 a.m.-
                 4:30 p.m.; closed Mondays

## How to get there:
BY CAR: The rugged road to the Oyster Farm goes left off Drake Highway .8 mile west of the turnoff to the Estero trailhead, at a small sign.

Anyone with the slightest liking for oysters will want to visit Johnson's. Anyone who has

The Estero Trail traverses moors and causeways above Home Bay

never tasted them—and I've known a surprising number of people who reached their mid-thirties without tasting one—should stop by here and risk getting addicted.

The narrow, rutted road leads a half mile to a jumble of houses, trailers, sheds, rusty machinery and mounds and mounds of oyster shells. A distinctive odor pervades the air, especially at low tide. Frequently on weekends companionable groups of oyster-buyers chat as they wait their turn at the shed that houses the retail sales room.

The Johnson Oyster Company is very much a family business, run by Charlie Johnson, his wife Makiko, and their sons and grandsons. Johnson learned his method of oyster farming (and met Makiko) in Japan. The oyster seedlings are planted on strings hanging from platforms in the bay. Thus suspended, they are safe from their natural predators, such as crabs and starfish, which inhabit the mud and silt below. The oysterlings flourish on the plankton of the unpolluted bay until they are ready for harvesting 18 months later. This method vastly increases production: nearly 80 per cent of the oysters survive, as opposed to 20-30 per cent of oysters grown on muddy bottoms. The Johnsons import seedlings from Washington State and Japan to replenish their stock.

The Johnsons have a long-term lease to continue oyster culture in about 1000 acres of the bay until the year 2015, so those of us who fancy the succulent bivalves can look forward to many more years of enjoyment. Incidentally, oysters are a relatively guilt-free treat: they are high in protein and low in calories, and contain desirable vitamins and minerals.

At the sales desk you can pick up a free leaflet that tells how the oysters are grown and gives recipes for them. For a real treat, you might bring along a barbecue, pick up your oysters in the shell, and repair to Drakes or Point Reyes Beach. Don't forget to bring: butter and/or lemon and/or barbecue sauce; a brush to clean the oysters before cooking; an oyster shucker or similar implement to open them; and a good Chardonnay if you are feeling flush, or a jug Chablis if you aren't. If you plan to purchase oysters in quantity, it's a good idea to phone ahead.

Sorting oysters from Drakes Estero at the Johnson Oyster Farm

56

# POINT REYES BEACH NORTH AND SOUTH

## How to get there:

BY CAR:  The road to Point Reyes Beach North is on the right, 2.7 miles west of the Oyster Company road. The road to Point Reyes Beach south is 2½ miles further along Drake. (The road to Drakes Beach is on the left, between the two Point Reyes Beach roads.)

Just west of the Oyster Company road, near the Coast Guard station sign, begins a mile-long lane of eucalyptus trees. These were planted around the turn of the century by a Swedish rancher, Captain Henry Claussen. The Coast Guard, Radio Corporation of America and American Telephone and Telegraph Company all maintain overseas radio receiving stations along the west side of this stretch of Drake Highway.

## Facilities:

Water, restrooms, picnic tables; dogs permitted.

## Regulations:

No swimming or wading because of the dangerous surf.

Point Reyes Beach, also called Ten Mile Beach or the Great Beach, is one long beach with two automobile entrances. It is one of the best places in the Bay Area to shake off urban malaise.

This wild and windy strand offers an exhilarating opportunity to run for miles. You can also walk the dog, or fish for perch, or make sculptures out of the abundant driftwood. During the winter you can watch for migrating whales.

If you come here on a foggy or stormy day, you can readily understand why so many shipwrecks took place on this beach, even after the lighthouse was built in 1870. The Coast Guard operated a lifesaving station here from 1888 until 1927, when it was moved to more sheltered Drakes Bay.

The local ranchers on occasion took part in rescue operations—as in 1861, when Carlyle S. Abbott saved all but one of the crew of the *Sea Nymph* by lassoing them as they struggled in the surf and tugging them ashore. The ranchers also took advantage of the salvage law to pick up cargo from abandoned ships. In 1874 the same Captain Claussen who planted the eucalyptus lane retrieved the figurehead of the New Zealand ship *Warrior Queen* and kept it prominently displayed on his ranch for many years. In 1885 Claussen swam to the abandoned English ship *Haddingtonshire*, rigged up a breeches buoy, and salvaged some of her cargo.

You can learn more about Point Reyes shipwrecks when you visit the lighthouse.

A ramble on Point Reyes Beach with only seagulls for company

# DRAKES BEACH

## How to get there
BY CAR: The turnoff is 2 miles south of the turnoff for Point Reyes Beach North.

## Facilities:
Water, restrooms and dressing rooms, picnic tables, grills. Visitor center open weekends and holidays 10 a.m.-4:30 p.m. (phone 669-1250). Snack bar open Friday through Tuesday 11 a.m.–4:30 p.m., "weather permitting."

## Regulations:
No dogs.

Looking at this tranquil, isolated spot, one would hardly guess that it is the center of a historical controversy that has aroused violent passions not only in California but around the world, and is still making headlines 400 years after the event that started it. To summarize briefly: In 1579, Francis Drake (who had not yet been knighted), having liberated a good deal of treasure from the Spaniards in the New World, was sailing along the California coast in search of a sheltered harbor where he could careen his weatherbeaten ship, the *Golden Hinde*, and make the repairs necessary for the voyage across the Pacific to the Orient and eventually back to England. On June 17 he found such a harbor; he brought the ship in and stayed until July 23.

Almost all we know about his visit is what we learn from an account presumably written by his chaplain, Francis Fletcher, because Drake's own log has not been seen since he presented it to Queen Elizabeth I upon his return. And even what we learn from Fletcher is secondhand: the first account relying on his journal was Richard Hakluyt's *The Famous Voyage of Sir Francis Drake into the South Sea*, published in 1589; the second was *The World Encompassed by Sir Francis Drake*, published in 1628—nearly 50 years after the event.

According to Fletcher, the harbor was "convenient and fit" but the climate was one of "thick mists and most stinking fogs." Drake called the place Nova Albion, partly because its white banks and cliffs reminded him of home. A large number of friendly Indians came to greet them and give them presents. Before leaving, Drake ceremonially took possession of the land in the name of Queen Elizabeth I, and nailed on a post a "plate of brass" inscribed to that effect.

Several generations of historians, both professional and amateur, have argued

The attractive Kenneth C. Patrick visitor center at Drakes Beach has ample parking space

fiercely over just where the *Golden Hinde* landed. In addition to Fletcher's account, they have a sketch map to go by: published in 1589 by a Flemish cartographer, Jodocus Hondius, it purports to show the port of Nova Albion.

This map is just as frustratingly vague as Fletcher's description, and at one time or another has been claimed to represent almost every bay in central and northern California. The majority of historians has long favored Drakes Bay as the landing place, but an articulate minority champions the northwest shore of San Francisco Bay. Bolinas Lagoon and Bodega and Tomales bays also have their partisans.

When a picnicker found what appeared to be Drake's original plate of brass near San Quentin Point in 1936, far from settling the question, it aroused even more controversy. If the plate were genuine, as metallurgical tests seemed to indicate, it would be powerful evidence in favor of San Francisco Bay. However, another man then came forth to state that he had picked up the plate near Drakes Bay and carried it around in his car for three years before finally throwing it out near San Quentin Point. And so the argument simmered on. Meanwhile, the plate of brass was ensconced in The Bancroft Library at the University of California, Berkeley, as one of that institution's most prized treasures.

In 1974, while some Drake fans were sailing from Plymouth, England, across the Atlantic in a painstakingly authentic replica of the *Golden Hinde*, the Drake controversy heated up again in the US. The California Historical Society devoted the entire fall issue of its *Quarterly* to a vigorous three-way debate among partisans of Drakes Estero, Bolinas Lagoon and San Quentin Cove as the landing place. Shortly thereafter, the prestigious historian Samuel Eliot Morison branded the plate of brass a fake, and suggested it might have been produced as an undergraduate prank.

Even before Morison's attack, the new Director of The Bancroft Library, Dr. James D. Hart, anticipating intensified interest in Drake as the quadricentennial of his landing approached, had arranged for further investigation of the plate. Techniques of metallurgy had become considerably more sophisticated in the nearly 40 years since the plate had been found. After scientists at Berkeley and Oxford subjected the plate to exhaustive analyses, Hart announced in 1977 that the

## ALONG SIR FRANCIS DRAKE HIGHWAY

An old rugged cross commemorates the first Anglican service in what is now the U.S., by Drake's chaplain in 1579

Lord Louis Mountbatten suggested that the British Navy contribute this anchor to mark the entrance to Drakes Estero

The quadricentennial of Drake's landing
attracts the navigator's admirers
to the visitor center

Gulls enjoy an al fresco lunch at Drakes Beach

tests strongly suggested that it was composed of modern metal rolled and cut in ways unknown in Drake's time. He added, with scholarly understatement but great prescience, that his report was "made with the recognition that this will probably not be accepted everywhere as the definitive or conclusive word on the subject."

The Bancroft report put the Elizabethan navigator on the front pages again, and the quadricentennial festivities kept him there. On June 16, 1979, the Sir Francis Drake Quadricentennial Committee of the Marin Coast Chamber of Commerce dedicated a bronze plaque near the south edge of the Drakes Beach parking lot, which reads: "On June 17, 1579, Captain Francis Drake sailed his ship *Golden Hinde* into the Gulf of the Farallones and the Bay that now bears his name. He sighted these white cliffs and named the land Nova Albion." A day earlier the Golden Gate National Recreation Area had dedicated a more noncommittal marker on Vista Point at the north end of the Golden Gate Bridge, stating "Historians have not yet agreed whether Drake's Marin County anchorage was in Drakes Estero, Bolinas Lagoon or San Francisco Bay." The California Historical Resources Commission couldn't agree to put a plaque *any*where.

The quadricentennial celebration was barely over when a completely novel argument enlivened the Drake controversy. As we noted on p. 18, Cermeno's Manila galleon was wrecked by a storm in Drakes Bay in 1595, and shards from her cargo of Ming porcelain subsequently turned up in excavations of Coast Miwok villages. Early in 1980 two scholars of porcelain studied almost 600 shards from the shores of Drakes Bay and concluded that they came from two entirely different shipments—one of them probably Drake's, since he was known to have looted some Ming porcelain from Spanish ships.

Anyone who has spent much time with Drakologists is well aware that it will take more than a few hundred pieces of china to settle this controversy. Much more incontrovertible evidence will be required—something like Drake's original log, if it should one day turn up in a long-neglected corner of the Tower of London or the Public Records Office, and if the paper, the ink, the handwriting and the wording could be certified as authentic by chemists, graphologists and linguists.

Even if you're firmly convinced that Drake really landed somewhere else, you'll still enjoy hiking up and down Drakes Beach, or just sunbathing on it. It's often less windy than the ocean beaches, and the quieter surf permits wading. You can also enjoy a leisurely stroll to examine the various Drake monuments that have been erected over the years. (When the visitor center is open, you can pick up a little guide to them.)

The oldest one is a rough-hewn granite cross under some Monterey pines and cypresses just north of the small picnic area adjoining the parking lot. Erected by the Sir

## ALONG SIR FRANCIS DRAKE HIGHWAY

Francis Drake Association of San Francisco in 1946, it commemorates the first Anglican church service held in what is now the United States, at which Chaplain Fletcher, the voyage's annalist, presided along with Drake.

At the south edge of the parking lot is the bronze plaque placed by the Sir Francis Drake Quadricentennial Committee of the Marin Coast Chamber of Commerce on June

Lake and dairy ranch above Drakes Beach

Rock formations on Drakes Beach look different each time sands shift around them

16, 1979, and dedicated by the Lord Bishop of London.

To reach the other monuments you walk east along the beach. (It is occasionally flooded at high tide. On weekends the visitor center posts tide tables.) The sand on Drakes Beach is constantly shifting with the tides and the seasons, and rocky shelves that may project three or four feet above the beach at one time you visit may be almost completely covered with sand another time.

A little over a mile from the parking lot, past the second bluff, when you see riffles in a channel ahead of you, look left to find a post about 12 feet high and less than ¼ mile away. You walk toward it (in spring, through mauve and violet lupine and golden fiddleneck) to find two more monuments. The old anchor, suggested by Lord Louis Mountbatten and donated by the Royal Navy, was erected by the Drake Navigators' Guild in 1954. Its accompanying sign states in no uncertain terms: "June 17, 1579, Francis Drake landed in this cove and here repaired his ship." Below the anchor a gray-black granite plaque placed by the guild in 1979 is somewhat more hesitant: "This cove is believed by many scholars to be the site of Sir Francis Drake's California harbor."

I had walked here alone late one afternoon to study the monuments. As I was transcribing their inscriptions, and musing on the enigmas of history, I was startled by a gunshot-loud SPLAT behind me. Whirling around, I discovered a harbor seal which had just flopped inelegantly into the estero and was swimming toward me. Behind him, lounging on a sandspit, was a colony of his fellows.

I walked through the tufts of bushy lupine to the shore and along it, followed in the water by the inquisitive seal. The mouth of the estero at low tide seemed barely deep

enough to admit even a canoe. We know, however, that ocean-going schooners regularly navigated it during the 19th century, so presumably Drake could have done so in the 16th.

It would indeed be exciting to have the Drake mystery solved beyond the shadow of a doubt, but then the great navigator might vanish forever from the front pages of our newspapers—and I, for one, find him much more agreeable than most of the 20th century phenomena I encounter there.

At low tide the rocks of Drakes Beach are a good place to look for tidepool creatures

### Recommended reading

Hanna, Warren, *Lost Harbor: The Controversy over Drake's California Anchorage*. Berkeley: University of California Press, 1979.

*The Plate of Brass Reexamined*. Berkeley: The Bancroft Library, University of California, 1977.

*The Plate of Brass Reexamined: Supplement*. Berkeley: The Bancroft Library, University of California, 1979.

The periodical literature is too abundant to cite here. Anyone who is interested should consult back files of the California Historical Society's journal, particularly the issue for Fall 1974.

# CHIMNEY ROCK

## How to get there

BY CAR: The turnoff is on the left, 3½ miles beyond the road to Point Reyes Beach South. A narrow road leads a mile to the main parking lot, passing another small parking lot along the way.

## Facilities:

Toilet at main parking lot.

The Coast Guard moved its life-saving station from the much stormier Point Reyes Beach to this more sheltered spot in 1927. New communications technology eventually rendered it obsolete, and in 1968 it was shut down. The remaining New England-style building below the parking lot is now a private residence. Commercial fishing boats frequent the bay offshore, especially during the salmon season.

A path leads from the main parking lot across windswept pasture to the promontory above Chimney Rock. On a clear day you can see down the coast all the way to San Francisco. To the north, the cliffs behind Drakes Bay resemble the White Cliffs of Dover more closely from this vantage point than from anywhere else in the Seashore—reminding us once again of Drake and Nova Albion. And, indeed, there is yet another monument to the great navigator here. To reach it, walk from the parking lot down around the old Coast Guard building. Across from the garage, beside the stairs leading to the building's front door, a bronze plaque declares unequivocally, "Francis Drake landed on these shores and took possession of the country, calling it Nova Albion." This monument was installed on June 17, 1950 (the 371st anniversary of Drake's landing) by the Yerba Buena chapter of E Clampus Vitus, a fraternal organization originally founded during Gold Rush days that is interested in California history.

Fishing pier at southwest end of Drakes Bay; remains of old life-saving station visible behind it

# THE LIGHTHOUSE

## How to get there

BY CAR: Continue on Drake Highway to its end, 21 miles beyond Bear Valley headquarters.

When whale watching burgeoned into a popular, indeed fashionable, activity in the early 1980s, the narrow road leading to the lighthouse frequently became seriously clogged on weekends. For a few years the Park Service instituted a shuttle bus route from Drakes Beach's parking lot to the lighthouse's, thereby greatly easing the congestion. Reductions in the NPS budget, however, made the shuttle bus economically unfeasible and it was cancelled. One weekend in 1984 as many as 14,000 whale watchers in 3500 cars attempted the journey to the lighthouse, producing virtual gridlock on the peninsula's bucolic road! It seems likely that the National Seashore will have to institute a reservation system for visiting the lighthouse on weekends during whale migration season, as Ano Nuevo State Park has done during elephant-seal breeding season.

## Facilities:

Water, restrooms; visitor center and lighthouse open Thursday through Monday 10-5:30 except when very foggy or windy (phone 669-1534).

## Regulations:

No dogs; stay on established trails and do not venture on hazardous cliffs.

The many shipwrecks on Point Reyes made a lighthouse a virtual necessity. Congress appropriated the money for it in 1852, but a protracted legal battle with the Shafter-Howard clan over the price of the land delayed construction for 18 years, during which period several more ships were wrecked. Finally, in 1870, the lighthouse was constructed, halfway down the 600-foot cliff. Why not at the top? Because while the Government was wrangling over the purchase of the Point Reyes land, the lighthouse service went ahead and built one at Point Bonita, north of the Golden Gate. They placed this light atop the cliff, but soon discovered that too often it was obscured by fog. Hence when they came to install the light at Point Reyes, they put it halfway down the cliff, even though this site greatly increased the expense and difficulty of con-

The stairs to the lighthouse have several platforms where visitors can rest and watch for whales

structing it and subsequently provisioning it. As a result, to visit the lighthouse you have to walk down stairs equivalent to a 30-story building—which isn't so bad, except that you then have to walk back up.

The old light, which was imported from France, is an extraordinarily complex and beautiful piece of machinery. (You can pick up a diagram of it at the visitor center.) Using only the light from four oil-burning

65

The Fresnel lens of the old lighthouse, made in Paris in 1867, has over a thousand pieces of glass

wicks, its intricate lens containing over a thousand pieces of glass enabled it to be seen 24 nautical miles out to sea.

Despite the light, and the installation of a foghorn in 1871, ships continued to be wrecked. Part of the problem was fog: Point Reyes is the foggiest spot on the Pacific Coast, and is second only to Nantucket Island in the whole United States. Another problem was that mariners mistook Point Reyes for the Golden Gate. One reason the shipwrecks produced relatively few fatalities was the installation of the Coast Guard Lifesaving Service, which operated on Point Reyes Beach from 1888 until 1927, when it was moved to Drakes Bay. Oddly enough, one of the most serious wrecks on the Point involved not a ship but a United Airlines DC-3 which crashed in 1938, killing five persons.

Life at the lighthouse in its early days was not easy. Just provisioning the place was a major undertaking, as you can imagine when you walk down the stairs to the light. Considering the keepers' isolation from society, the terrible weather they had to contend with, and the din of the foghorn—sometimes going on for days—it is not surprising that insubordination and drunkenness were frequent, and that in 1889 an assistant "went crazy and was handed over to the constable in Olema."

Since those days both the light and the foghorn have benefited from technical improvements that made duty easier for the keepers who manned them. In 1975 a new light was installed, one that is automated by a computer. The old light is still operable, however, just in case the computer should ever fail. The Coast Guard closed the lighthouse to the public in 1967 because it lacked personnel to oversee visitors on the then-hazardous stairs. After automation, the Coast Guard turned the lighthouse over to the National Park Service, which reopened it to the public in 1977.

Before you walk the quarter mile to the lighthouse, take the short trail from the parking lot to the sea lion overlook. The trail leads through a veritable garden of succulents plus buckwheat, lizardtail, seaside daisy, paintbrush, yarrow, phacelia and the ubiquitous lupine and poppy. From the over-

## Recommended reading

*The Point Reyes Light.* Coastal Parks Association, 1979. Paperback booklet on sale at the visitor center.

look you can frequently see and hear sea lions on the rocks below.

The road from the parking lot to the lighthouse leads past cypress trees and more flowers, and on clear days affords a view of the Great Beach and north to Bodega Head. Of course in winter you will be keeping your eyes open for migrating whales. The search for whales can also occupy you during the long trek down the stairs, and the even longer one back up. The park service has considerately provided rest stops at intervals. When the whales are not running, you can entertain yourself by studying the myriad of succulents and wildflowers along the stairs and the colorful lichen on the rocks. The rocks themselves near the visitor center represent what geologist Alan Galloway refers to as "fine exposures of coarse Paleocene conglomerate" and "interesting sedimentary structures."

An elaborate clockwork mechanism, powered by weights, turns the old light's lens assembly on brass trunnions

# ALONG PIERCE POINT ROAD

Although the road is officially called *Pierce Point*, the point itself appears on most maps as *Tomales*. The road is named for Solomon Pierce, who in 1858 bought 2200 acres on the point and established a model dairy ranch. As Jack Mason describes it in *Point Reyes: The Solemn Land*, it must have been impressive indeed: in addition to 300 cows, it contained "a blacksmith shop, model cow and horse barns, a carpenter shop where butter boxes were made, a schoolhouse, a laundry with a Chinese in charge, and a warehouse stocked with sugar, tea, syrups, flour and other provender that reminded one visitor of a country store." After being in the Pierce family's possession for three generations, the ranch was bought by James McClure in 1929.

Pierce Point Road runs across some of the wildest country on the Point Reyes peninsula. After you leave the bishop pines of Tomales Bay State Park, there are few trees and you can see for miles over the moors and out to sea. One might consider the landscape almost desolate were it not for the occasional substantial-looking ranch houses and the multitude of cattle. The pungent odor of manure often drifts through the car window. This is good birding country: crows, ravens and vultures are much in evidence, and hawks perch on the fences and telephone poles near the road. Often they will let you get surprisingly close to them.

## TOMALES BAY STATE PARK

**Phone:**   669-1140

### How to get there:

BY CAR: From Inverness drive west and then south on Sir Francis Drake Highway for 2½ miles to Pierce Point Road and turn onto it. The main entrance to the park is a little over a mile from the Drake Highway junction.

If all you want to do in the park is hike, not swim or picnic, you can sometimes find a (free) parking place in the clearing 350 yards south of the main entrance; the Jepson Trail, described below, takes off from here, and so does the 3-mile-long trail to Shell Beach.

Shell Beach, although part of the state park—in fact, the oldest part of it—is separated from the park's other beaches by a

A covey of California quail, the state bird, along the side of Pierce Point Road

A sailboat at Pebble Beach

Steller's sea lions lounging on rocks
north of McClures Beach

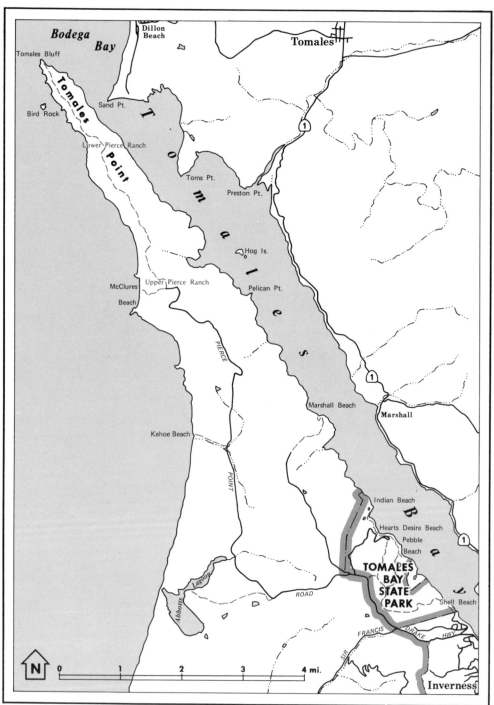

**ALONG PIERCE POINT ROAD**
MAP 6

**LEGEND:**

——— Roads
- - - - Trail
▬▬▬ Park Bdy.
◉ Campground

patch of private land. In the summer of 1980 a youth conservation group constructed a trail linking Shell with the other beaches, and it is described at the end of this section. Drivers, however, must still approach Shell by the traditional route: From Inverness, drive north on Drake Highway, turn right on Camino del Mar and follow it to the small parking lot at its end. From here you have to walk about a quarter mile through oak and madrone woodland to the beach. Actually, Shell consists of two beaches. To reach Shell II you walk another quarter mile north of Shell I. Both beaches are extremely attractive and are much favored by the local residents.

## Facilities:
Water, restrooms and dressing rooms, picnic tables, grills; about 20 bicycle campsites. Hand-carried boats may be put in the water away from the swimming beaches. Map available from ranger station for a small price.

## Regulations:
$2 day-use fee per car; dogs not permitted on beaches or trails or in the natural areas of the park.

Tomales Bay State Park antedates Point Reyes National Seashore by a full decade. In fact, it was the threat of private development on the bayfront here that first spurred conservationist militance in the Point Reyes area. In 1945 a group led by the Marin Conservation League purchased 185 acres at Shell Beach for $30,000 (about what one acre of unimproved land sells for in the Inverness area now; obviously, they got there at the right time). In 1951 a combination of private contributors, conservationist groups and the state purchased another 840 acres, and a year later the state took over both parcels as a park. It remains a sort of enclave within the National Seashore.

This charming park is sometimes a sunny refuge when the rest of the peninsula is fogged in. Its small, sheltered beaches are a pleasant contrast to the windswept ones on the rest of the peninsula, and for swimmers Tomales Bay is milder and warmer than Drakes Bay—let alone the Pacific Ocean. (There is no lifeguard service, however.) The picnic area is unusually attractive, containing many tables screened by lush foliage and offering splendid views across the bay.

**Picknickers at one of the pleasant sites of Tomales Bay State Park**

71

From the parking lot at Hearts Desire Beach, short trails lead north over the forested bluffs to Indian Beach and south to Pebble Beach. Children will enjoy these walks from beach to beach, and will see why the Coast Miwok Indians were so fond of this area. Fishing and clamming were popular with the Indians, and still are; but unlike the original inhabitants, you will have to obtain a fishing license before you arrive.

A delightful loop hike of a bit under 3 miles can be made by combining the Jepson and Johnstone trails. This hike is enjoyable at almost any time of year, in almost any weather short of a driving rainstorm. To start it from Hearts Desire Beach, take the trail leading to Pebble Beach. It traverses the picnic area and just before actually reaching the beach connects with the Johnstone Trail (named for the late Bruce Johnstone, a leading Marin conservationist). The trail ascends gradually through luxuriant shrubbery, ferns and picturesque trees. The park service has recycled some of its former signs to create footbridges over occasional streamlets.

A mile from Pebble Beach, the Johnstone Trail arrives at a gravel road. If you go uphill on the road for ¼ mile you come to a locked vehicle gate and the unofficial free parking lot mentioned above. To finish your loop back to Hearts Desire Beach, take the (signed) Jepson Trail. This trail is named for the late botanist Willis Linn Jepson, founder of the UC School of Forestry and author of the monumental *Manual of the Flowering Plants of California*. The trail goes through the Jepson Memorial Grove of bishop pines. As we noted in the Introduction, the Point Reyes peninsula is one of the very few places where this ancient species of pine flourishes. Occasional well-sited benches invite the hiker to rest and contemplate the view through pines, oaks and madrones over Tomales Bay. After a mile in the verdant forest, you arrive again at the main parking lot.

Jogging through the forest on the Jepson Trail

For a longer hike, you can try the trail built by a youth conservation group in the summer of 1980 that connects Hearts Desire and Shell beaches, bypassing the private land between them. This is a hike of about four miles each way (not counting the half mile to the Shell Beach parking lot). One possibility is for the swimmers in your group to drop off the hikers at one end of the trail and take the car to the other end.

To get on this trail, simply cross the paved road at the south end of the Johnstone Trail.

An access trail from the south end of the Jepson Trail also leads to it. The trail contours at an elevation of about 500 feet, through salal, ferns, huckleberry and bishop pines. Once in a while a break in the forest permits a view of Tomales Bay.

After a couple of miles the trail begins to descend gradually through tanoak and madrone, and comes out at Shell Beach II. If you're hiking in the other direction, you can pick up this trail at the north end of the beach, near the garbage cans.

## MARSHALL BEACH

### How to get there
BY CAR: The road leading to Marshall Beach begins just beyond the road to Tomales Bay State Park, at a sign *L Ranch*. It runs past private property over moors for 2½ miles to a primitive parking lot. From here a trail leads 1½ miles down to the beach.

### Facilities:
Toilets at beach.

### Regulations:
No dogs, camping or motor vehicles.

This is a delightful little beach sheltered by ancient cypresses. Frankly, however, it is not in my opinion so delightful that I would choose to walk a mile and a half over rather

bleak pasture land, past mistrustful-looking cows, to reach it. I've been there by foot and I've been there by boat, and by boat is better. As the Golden Hinde Boatel in Inverness no longer rents boats, try to strike up an acquaintance with someone who keeps a boat moored on Tomales Bay!

## ABBOTTS LAGOON

### How to get there
BY CAR: The small parking lot is 2 miles beyond the turnoff to Tomales Bay State Park.

### Facilities:
Toilets at parking lot. Swimming is possible in the lagoon, but not the ocean. The lagoon is large enough so that you can canoe in it, if you're willing to portage the canoe a few hundred feet from the parking lot and subsequently over the natural dam separating the two parts of the lagoon.

### Regulations:
Dogs on leash permitted; no camping or motor vehicles.

The Abbott brothers were ranchers here in the 1860s. It was one of them, Carlyle, who saved all the crew but the steward from the wrecked clipper *Sea Nymph* in 1861 by lasso-

**Beachcombing between Abbotts Lagoon and Kehoe Beach**

ing them one at a time with his riata and pulling them ashore. (The *Sea Nymph* was one of several ships that mistook Point Reyes for the Golden Gate in the fog.)

The trail to the lagoon, an old ranch road, begins at a hiker's stile and runs across open pasture through another one. In a short mile you arrive at the narrow passage between the upper and lower parts of the lagoon. A bridge crosses over to the sand dune on the other side.

Now you can walk across the dunes toward the ocean. A glorious sweep of clean driftwood beach stretches for miles in either direction. Since it is impossible to reach this spot without walking at least a mile, you can be sure that the strand will be blissfully uncrowded. A low sandbar normally separates the lagoon from the ocean, but during heavy storms the waves occasionally wash over it.

The lagoon and the beach are both fascinating to birders, especially during the fall migrations. Animal fanciers may catch a glimpse of the goats that inhabit the hill behind the lagoon.

## KEHOE BEACH

### How to get there
BY CAR: The small parking lot is 2 miles north of Abbotts Lagoon parking lot. (People often have to park on the roadside.)

### Facilities:
Toilets at parking lot.

Hikers on the way to Kehoe Beach

74

## Regulations:

No swimming or wading because of the dangerous surf. Dogs on leash permitted on beach.

The path to the beach leads along a creek running through a swampy area. Soon you reach a small lagoon. Winter storms pile up driftwood logs here in wild formations. A half mile from the parking lot you arrive at the white sandy beach. Kehoe is actually the northern end of the strand that is variously called Point Reyes Beach, the Great Beach, and Ten Mile, Eleven Mile and Twelve Mile Beach. You can walk south almost as far as the lighthouse, but to the north your passage is blocked about a mile from the entrance trail by granite cliffs jutting into the ocean.

You can also stretch your legs by hiking on the bluffs above the beach. An obvious trail leads off from the right of the entrance trail just before you get to the beach. You can wander over cowpaths or cross-country (being careful not to go too close to the edge of the cliff). These hillsides are a mass of wildflowers in, spring—baby blue eyes, suncups, wild hollyhock and iris. In winter, the cliffs offer a good vantage point to watch for whales.

## McCLURES BEACH

### How to get there

BY CAR: Drive to the end of Pierce Point Road, about 9 miles from the Drake Highway Junction.

### Facilities:

Toilets at parking lot; phone.

### Regulations:

No dogs; no swimming or wading because of the dangerous surf.

Like Kehoe Beach, McClures is reached by a half-mile-long trail from the parking lot; and as at Kehoe, the trail follows the course of a stream. Growing on the bank to your right as you walk down are buckwheat, morning glory, lizardtail and gumweed.

The beautiful beach is less than a mile long, being blocked at either end by unclimbable granite cliffs projecting into the ocean. At low tide you can walk through a

defile in the rocks at the south end to a pocket beach. Here you may see cormorants perched on Elephant Rock and the other offshore stacks. Exploring tidepool life is another popular activity at McClures Beach.

Hiking along Kehoe Beach

Oystercatchers enjoy tidepooling at McClures Beach

# TOMALES POINT (PIERCE POINT) TRAIL

### How to get there
BY CAR: The trailhead is at Upper Pierce Ranch.

### Facilities:
No water along the route; toilets, phone at McClures Beach parking lot.

### Regulations:
No dogs.

Most of this trail is actually the old road that linked the upper and lower model dairy ranches operated by the Pierce family for three generations (see p. 68). The point is now home to a herd of tule elk relocated from Owens Valley, which have displaced the former cattle.

The trip to the end of the point is about 8 km (5 miles) long. It's quite level, highly scenic, entirely open, and often windy and foggy. Bring a waterproof windbreaker, plus binoculars if you own them.

From the ranch, the road ascends gradually for a mile. You can look down over McClures Beach and the inaccessible beach to its north. On one occasion as I walked along here I saw, many miles out to sea, what looked like a group of gigantic aircraft carriers. I debated whether I should run back to the parking lot screaming "Invasion! Invasion!," before I decided that an unusual combination of light and water had created a peculiar mirage out of the Farallon Islands and their reflections.

As the road continues its gentle ascent, it passes granitic outcroppings on the low hills. If your imagination is running wild—as mine was after viewing the phantom fleet—you can easily fancy that these are ancient Celtic tumuli, from which a Druid or one of the Little People might pop up at any moment. The eeriness of the scene is heightened when you discover a line of boulders running perfectly straight, almost due north and south, on either side of the road as far as the eye can see.

As you walk along, you enjoy superb and ever-changing views of Tomales Bay. Just offshore to the east is two-plus-acre Hog Island. According to historian Jack Mason's *Earthquake Bay*, "By most accounts it got its name when a barge broke loose, depositing its cargo of porkers on the beach." In the

Trail north of McClures Beach overlooks a wild coastline of eroded cliffs and off-shore rocks

A pocket beach on Tomales Point

19th century a succession of German families lived on the island, and the remains of a house are still there. Somewhere along the line, the island got forested with eucalyptus—obviously not its natural vegetation. The Audubon Society acquired it in 1972, and it will continue in its present state, uninhabited but a magnet to daytime visitors in kayaks, canoes and sailboats. White Gulch, an inlet on the shore just west of Hog Island, was the site of the Tomales Point Gun Club from 1904 to 1941. Herbert Hoover was one of its distinguished guests.

Across Tomales Bay you can see Toms Point and to its north Sand Point, with the village of Dillon Beach on the slope above it. Still farther north is Bodega Head. On the right side of Sand Point is Lawson's Landing, which consists mainly of a huge trailer park. The dunes above it are occasionally frequented by hang gliders, and one afternoon as we lunched atop a Tomales Point hillock we watched a few dozen boldly colored gliders seeking vainly for a favorable wind, only to plunge ignominiously back into the dunes.

Now the road descends gradually toward Lower Pierce Ranch, passes a pond and an old corral, and peters out into a trail. About a mile beyond the ranch it arrives at a bluff just across from Bird Rock, a large offshore stack usually inhabited by cormorants. One New Year's Day a group of us hiked here hoping to see migrating whales; we drew a blank on whales, but instead saw a huge flock of white pelicans on Bird Rock. A path leads down the steep 200-foot cliff to a small beach here; *only the agile and surefooted should attempt this climb.* (Ill-coordinated acrophobes will not even be tempted.)

From Bird Rock to the end of the point is less than a mile. The trail more or less disappears in a broad patch of sand, but you can proceed cross-country to the bluff overlooking the entrance to Tomales Bay. Here you can lounge at leisure with your lunch, watching boats and looking for seals and interesting birds, to the accompaniment of the plangent, faintly melancholy clang of a bell buoy.

On the hike mentioned above, the air was so clear at the bluff that looking southeast we could see Mt. Tamalpais in the distance above Hog Island; but by the time we had retraced our steps as far as Lower Pierce Ranch fog had completely enveloped us, and by the time we reached the parking lot those of us who had not brought along waterproof windbreakers were completely soaked. This sort of rapid, unpredictable weather change is par for the course on Tomales Point, and one should come prepared.

Heading for the tip of Tomales Point, with Bodega Head visible to the north

## How to get there

BY CAR:   The trailhead is just off Highway 1, 3½ miles south of Olema. (There is a private ranch called Five Brooks a bit north of the *actual* trailhead, which is marked by a sign in Seashore blue and white.) Coming north on Highway 1, Five Brooks is about 5 miles beyond the turnoff to Bolinas.

## Facilities:

Water, toilets, a few picnic tables. There is no water on most of the trails around here.

## Regulations:

No dogs on trails; no open fires, no motor vehicles, no firearms; camping by permit only, free at Bear Valley headquarters.

Geologist Alan Galloway points out: "At Five Brooks, as the name implies, the drainage is very complex and is undoubtedly affected by fault movements. . . Olema Creek and Pine Gulch Creek run parallel to one another in opposite directions, separated only by about 1500 feet. . ." Some of the trails from Five Brooks lead along these capricious creeks; others ascend Inverness Ridge and run along it. Logging took place in parts of this forest as late as the 1950s, but nature is now reclaiming her own as young trees sprout up.

This southern part of the park is full of old trails that are unmaintained, unsigned and unmapped. The main hazard in venturing on them is poison oak.

### RIFT ZONE TRAIL

One of the most attractive trails out of Five Brooks is the 5-mile-long Rift Zone Trail running north to Bear Valley. This trail is described in pp. 36-37. To get on it from the Five Brooks end, head north from the parking lot past a pond fringed with willows, and in less than 100 yards bear right on a path signed *Bear Valley Trail Through Vedanta Retreat.*

### TRAILS TO FIRTOP AND BEYOND

Most of the trails in the Five Brooks area are reached by circling counterclockwise around the duck pond near the parking lot. (On one occasion we saw a large turtle sunning himself

Turtles are sometimes seen sunbathing on a log in the pond at the Five Brooks Trailhead

Young second-growth firs line the Glen Camp Trail west of Firtop

The Greenpicker Trail out of Five Brooks is popular with equestrians on a rock in this pond.) At a fork, signs point the way to Palomarin on the left and Bear Valley on the right. To get to Firtop, go right on the signed Stewart Trail. This is an old logging road that climbs gradually up through ferny forest, crossing one of the five brooks on its way. After about a mile you reach a junction with the Greenpicker Trail, and now you can choose which way to proceed to Firtop.

The Stewart Trail is somewhat more gradual. After a couple of miles it emerges on the Ridge Trail. From here you turn right to reach Firtop in less than a mile. The Greenpicker Trail is somewhat shorter, steeper and narrower—more of a true trail. Part of it climbs along the edge of the Vedanta Society's retreat. It levels off in a corridor of young Douglas firs to reach Firtop.

Firtop (1324') is a broad, level meadow surrounded by fir trees. It's a pleasant place for lunch, and if you have enough to eat, drink and read you might want to spend the afternoon here. Firtop is also a major trail junction, offering several options:

You can return to Five Brooks via whichever trail you did not take coming up.

You can take the gently rolling Ridge Trail for a mile and a half to a three-way junction in a parklike forest, and turn left on the Bolema Trail. It runs steeply down the ridge and turns left to return to Five Brooks. (This would constitute a loop of about 7 miles.)

If you want something more strenuous, or if you can arrange a car shuttle, you can take the unnamed old road that runs south from Firtop. It descends rather steeply through fir forest and turns west to arrive at a signed trail junction. Here you can choose whether to go right, to Bear Valley (by way of Glen Camp if desired); or left, descending steeply to Wildcat Camp. From Wildcat it's 5 miles to the Palomarin trailhead. Either of those routes will take most hikers a full day.

Double Point as seen from the Lake Ranch Trail south of Firtop

This trail might be considered a continuation of the Rift Zone Trail. Like the Rift Zone Trail, the Olema Valley Trail runs for about 5 fairly level miles along the San Andreas fault zone through a delightful mixture of forest and farmland.

Like the Rift Zone Trail, the Olema Valley Trail would probably be more popular with hikers if the park service routed a shuttle bus along Highway 1. As it is, you have to retrace your steps, or make a long, strenuous loop involving the Ridge Trail, or arrange your own two-car shuttle. For a 5-mile hike, take both cars to the southern end of the trail, 4¼ miles south of the Five Brooks turnoff (if driving north, a long half mile north of Horseshoe Hill Road). A sign on the west side of Highway 1 announces the Olema Valley Trail, and just across the highway another sign announces the McCurdy Trail going up Bolinas Ridge in GGNRA land. The road here is wide enough for a few cars to park. Leave one here and take the other car to Five Brooks.

(The official map name of the community near the southern end of the trail is Woodville, but it is frequently called by its original name, Dogtown. In the 1850s and '60s this was a rip-roaring lumbering town. In 1868 its citizens, hoping to attract marriageable women, officially changed its name to the more genteel Woodville.)

From Five Brooks trailhead turn left at the fountain—that is, the circular horse fountain commemorating "Sonny" Zappetini, a San Rafael ironworker and dedicated horseman. Walk clockwise around the duck pond and when the graveled road curves right, go left on the signed Bolema Trail. It begins as a broad, level, leafy path, at times under a virtual tunnel of alders.

After crossing a creek on a culvert, the trail climbs for a half mile—the only steep part of this walk. A little over a mile from the trailhead you reach a signed junction; the Bolema Trail continues uphill to join the Ridge Trail, while the Olema Valley Trail goes downhill to the left. Soon you turn right at a hiker's symbol to go through a fence gate.

Now the broad path undulates over old fields dotted with Douglas firs and coyote brush. You can look over the ranches to Bolinas Ridge on the east. Just before you reach a cypress windbreak, a hiker's symbol advises you to bear right, and a sign informs you that you are halfway through the 5-mile jaunt. The path switchbacks abruptly, then continues running south. Eventually it turns into a true trail, rather than a broad wagon track, as it traverses a pleasant forest of oaks and bays alternating with grassy glades.

During much of this journey you have been walking between the two streams that geologist Alan Galloway cites as examples of the fault zone's complex drainage system: "In this area, Olema Creek and Pine Gulch Creek run parallel to one another in opposite directions, separated only by about 1500 feet, with Olema Creek flowing into Tomales Bay to the north and Pine Gulch Creek into Bolinas Lagoon to the south." And a look at the USGS maps will reveal that many of the streams make odd right-angle bends when they reach the fault zone. By this point on the trail you can hear Pine Gulch Creek bubbling merrily on your right, oblivious to its geologic peculiarity, and soon you ford two of its tributaries. The trail goes through a gate and across a field behind a handsome farmhouse. Just before it goes through another gate, a sign points out the way to Pablo Point. Energetic hikers might want to take this trail up to the top of Inverness Ridge and loop back to Five Brooks by the Ridge Trail—about 12 miles altogether, including the 4½ already covered.

The Olema Valley Trail now fords yet another creek and skirts a large marsh. It runs near the edge of the highway, then crosses another field to reach the Dogtown trailhead.

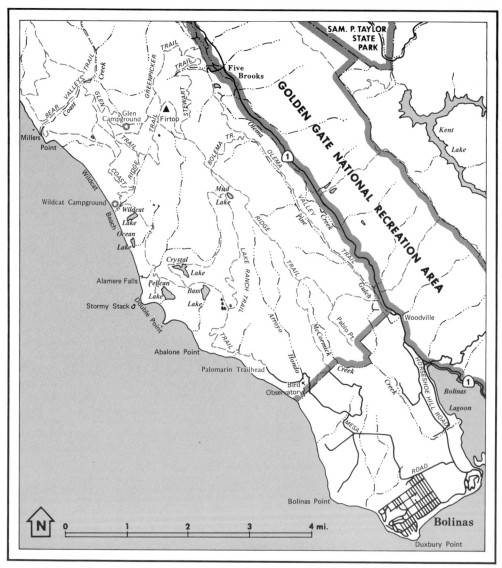

SAM. P. TAYLOR STATE PARK

GOLDEN GATE NATIONAL RECREATION AREA

Five Brooks

BEAR VALLEY TRAIL

GREENPICKER TRAIL

STEWART TRAIL

Coast Creek

GLEN TRAIL

Glen Campground

Firtop

COAST RIDGE TRAIL

Millers Point

Wildcat Beach

Wildcat Campground

Wildcat Lake

Ocean Lake

BOLEMA TR.

OLEMA

Kent Lake

Mud Lake

RIDGE TRAIL

Crystal Lake

Pelican Lake

LAKE RANCH TRAIL

Alamere Falls

Bass Lake

Stormy Stack

Double Point

Abalone Point

Palomarin Trailhead

Bird Observatory

TRAIL

Arroyo

Hondo

McCormick

Pablo Pt.

Pine Gulch

Creek

Woodville

Creek

HORSESHOE HILL ROAD

Bolinas Lagoon

MESA

ROAD

Bolinas Point

ROAD

Bolinas

Duxbury Point

N  0    1    2    3    4 mi.

**TRAILS FROM FIVE BROOKS AND PALOMARIN**
## MAP 7

LEGEND:

Roads
Trail
Park Bdy.
⊙ Campground

**Occasionally hikers are fortunate enough
to encounter a badger
at his front door**

## How to get there

**BY CAR:**

NORTHBOUND: From Stinson Beach proceed north on Highway 1 for 4½ miles and at the Bolinas turnoff go left for 1¾ miles to Mesa Road, on your right, before reaching Bolinas proper. Follow Mesa to its end, 4½ miles north. Along the way you pass the RCA Communications Center, with towers that look like artifacts from Alpha Centauri; a windowless, half-sunken Coast Guard station with a slightly sinister aspect; and the remains of the buildings once occupied by a religious commune, the Church of the Golden Rule, whose members lived here in self-sufficient isolation.

SOUTHBOUND: From Olema go south on Highway 1 for 8 miles to Horseshoe Hill Road, go right, proceed for 2 miles to Mesa Road, and follow it to the end as described above.

# PALOMARIN AND WILDCAT CAMP

## Facilities:

Toilets ¼ mile from the trailhead. Phone at Point Reyes Bird Observatory. Dogs permitted at Palomarin Beach but not on trails. Wildcat Camp has water, toilets, picnic tables, grills and hitchrails.

## Regulations:

The usual: No dogs on trails; no open fires, no motor vehicles, no firearms; camping by permit only, free at Bear Valley headquarters. Wildcat Camp is generally reserved for groups, but individuals and families may camp here in sites that groups have not reserved.

Campers at Wildcat have miles of unspoiled beach to explore

# POINT REYES
## BIRD OBSERVATORY AND PALOMARIN BEACH

Point Reyes Bird Observatory is a nonprofit, membership-supported organization devoted to the study and conservation of wildlife—particularly seabirds, landbirds and marine mammals. One of its most valuable functions is to act as guardian for the Farallon Islands 20 miles offshore. The Farallones support the largest seabird colony in the continental United States, as well as a sizable population of seals and sea lions. Before the PRBO took them under its wing, so to speak, these birds and animals were being hunted and harassed by humans.

The observatory is open to the public free from dawn to dusk. It contains some ornithological exhibits, and if you arrive at the right time in the morning you might be able to watch the staff banding birds.

Palomarin Beach, ½ mile west of the observatory, is one of the places in the Seashore you can take your dog. To reach the narrow beach you must walk about a mile down a graveled road.

## COAST TRAIL
## TO WILDCAT CAMP

Wildcat Camp is a possible overnight backpack stop and an excellent goal for an all-day hike. The trail to it passes four freshwater lakes, and a fifth is reachable by an easy side trip. These lakes testify to the area's geologic instability, which results from its proximity to the San Andreas Fault: They were formed by earth slippages that blocked the natural drainage. (In fact, the whole Palomarin area might be considered one huge landslide.)

Wildcat Camp, like Coast, is open and treeless; its charm is its situation a few hundred feet from a splendid, uncrowded beach. (Any beach, however magnificent, that requires five miles or more of hiking to reach is going to be uncrowded most of the time.)

From the parking lot, full of colorful weeds in spring and summer, head for a eucalyptus grove across a little gully full of paintbrush, morning glory, lupine and poison hemlock. Trail signs give mileages to various spots and the list of regulations. The toilets are just past the signs. As you leave the eucalyptus grove, an obvious shortcut trail begins to the right of a cypress. Soon the shortcut rejoins the main Coast Trail, an old farm road that

**A bird in the hand is being weighed at the Point Reyes Bird Observatory**

**Backpackers slog north on the Coast Trail heading for Wildcat Camp**

runs along the headlands a couple of hundred feet above the ocean. For the next 2 miles you will be walking mainly through coastal scrub—e.g., coyote brush, California sagebrush and poison oak. There is a somewhat melancholy cast to this country, especially on a cloudy day. However, if you take the hike in spring or summer, any tendency toward gloom may be dispelled by the profusion of flowers. Along the headlands are red and yellow paintbrush, common and dwarf brodiaea, morning glory, wild cucumber and assorted members of the sunflower family. As the season progresses, you can find clarkia, coast buckwheat, pearly everlasting and masses of lizardtail.

After ½ mile the trail goes briefly into a little gully containing a stream. It returns to the cliffs; then a mile from the trailhead it leaves the ocean and crosses another stream graced by watercress, yellow monkey flower and brass buttons. Now you ascend gradually along the north side of a canyon, pass through a defile among Ithuriel's spear, tidytips and yarrow, and descend past the Lake Ranch Trail (sign) on the right. On the left, several ponds mark the site where the old ranch house stood. They attract kildeer, swallows and huge flocks of red-winged blackbirds.

Now the trail levels off, then descends gradually through alders and willows, and soon passes sheltered Bass Lake. You are not likely to find bass here, but you might find trout—and in warm weather, a few skinny-dippers. A quarter mile beyond Bass Lake, a side trail to Crystal Lake branches off to the right. (On my most recent visit to this lake, it was so full of algae that its name seemed a perverse joke.) The next lake is triangular Pelican, below you to the left. As the trail leaves the lake, you can see on a clear day the whole Point Reyes peninsula spread out before you, with the stacks off Miller Point in the middle distance.

From Pelican Lake the trail descends gently, following signs with a hiker's symbol. Two side roads go off to the left to overlook Double Point and Stormy Stack—worth a side trip for the superb ocean view and a chance of seeing seals. The main Coast Trail crosses Alamere Creek. When you reach a **Y**, where the right branch is signed *Wildcat Camp* and the left *Wildcat Beach*, bear left toward the ocean, which soon becomes audible again. Passing the sign pointing out the beach-access trail on the left, you soon come to marshy Ocean Lake on the right. Now the trail climbs steeply for ¼ mile along a cliff overlooking the sea, the peninsula and, to the right, Wildcat Lake. From here you descend to the camp.

You can make part of your return journey by way of the beach: Walk south toward Double Point, which as you approach it from this angle has a surprising resemblance to the Rock of Gibraltar. You are also approaching Alamere Falls, to which you can make a side trip. The access route back to the Coast Trail begins a short mile south of Wildcat Camp.

Trail riders taking a break at Wildcat Camp

# THE LAKE RANCH AND RIDGE TRAILS

Here is a scenic 11-mile all-day loop that covers a lot of diverse terrain. If you can arrange a two-car shuttle, you can make it a one-way 7½-mile hike by leaving one car at Five Brooks trailhead and finishing on the Bolema Trail rather than the Ridge Trail.

For the first 2 miles, follow the Coast Trail, as in the previous section. Turn right on the Lake Ranch Trail—which, like so many in the national seashore, is an old farm road—and begin a steady ascent through coastal scrub. As you climb, you get ever-widening views of the peninsula, and soon you can see jewel-like Bass, Pelican and Crystal lakes shimmering beneath you.

The trail levels off in a delightful, grassy area frequented by giant jackrabbits. After two miles the Lake Ranch Trail enters a cool, shady Douglas-fir forest. Soon you pass Mud Lake, a tarn full of tule and azolla, or water fern. As one of the more bizarre effects of the 1906 quake, this lake was almost completely drained. Harold Gilliam notes, "The only clue as to what happened was that a spring on the east side of the ridge three quarters of a mile away suddenly increased greatly in volume. Since the quake, the lake has been restored by natural processes."

Shortly after passing Mud Lake you come to a four-way trail junction (sign) at a rustic old gate in an almost parklike forest. This is an idyllic lunch spot. If you left one car at Five Brooks, you can reach it by taking the Bolema Trail, which runs northeast from this junction for 2½ miles down to that trailhead. Otherwise, turn southeast on the Ridge Trail, which ascends gently along the crest of the ridge. The area east of the trail was obviously logged earlier in this century, and now you can look over the stumps to Mt. St. Helena. After a mile or so, the fir forest becomes dense again, and beneath the trees grow lots of sword fern and huckleberry—in late summer you might harvest enough for a pie. After 2½ miles on the Ridge Trail you come to a sign indicating a possible side trip (1¾ miles each way) to Pablo Point.

The Ridge Trail now begins to descend, and emerges from the forest. Soon you can see the ocean on the right and the exposed ridge of Pablo Point on the other side of a very deep gorge on the left, then toylike Stinson Beach far below and eventually the City gleaming in the distance—always assuming, of course, that the fog hasn't come in. The last mile of descent, fairly steep, brings you out on the road near the bird observatory. Turn right here and walk the mile back to the trailhead.

**A four-foot-high pack-rat nest near the trail south of Glen Camp**

**The Lake Ranch Trail near its junction with the Ridge Trail, above Mud Lake**

**Some of the Ridge Trail is a level road once used for lumbering**

# SAFETY AND SELF-PROTECTION FOR HIKERS AND DRIVERS

For almost two years a murderer whom the media dubbed "The Trailside Killer" terrorized the entire Bay Area by attacking hikers, mostly women, at random in such popular parks as Mt. Tamalpais and Point Reyes National Seashore. After another killing in a Santa Cruz County park, a suspect was finally captured, and he has now disappeared into the exceedingly slow mills of the judicial system. Meanwhile, the trailside killings have apparently ceased. As the weekly "Sheriff's Calls" in the *Point Reyes Light* demonstrate, however, crime has not yet vanished from West Marin. In particular, nearly every issue records an incident of "car clouting"—the theft of wallets, cameras, jewelry, clothing, camping gear and/or other valuables from cars parked along roadsides or even in busy lots.

*Always leave cars locked with windows securely closed*, and never leave valuable objects visible within. Better yet, leave all valuable objects at home.

If you want to go hiking, running, bicycling or canoeing with utmost safety, *go with a group*. If you ask the rangers at National Seashore headquarters (663-1092), they will tell you when groups are meeting to go hiking, jogging, and so forth. Or they will help you form your own group. On p. 25 of this book is a list of organizations that regularly conduct outings in Point Reyes National Seashore and elsewhere in the Bay Area. The one that leads by far the most walks is the Sierra Club, which offers several excursions every weekend—some of them quite suitable for tenderfeet. You need not be a member to join the outings, and visitors from out of town are welcome. Just get in touch with them:

National Headquarters
530 Bush Street
San Francisco 94108
981-8634

San Francisco Bay Chapter
6014 College Avenue
Oakland 94618
658-7470

Marin County Regional Group
P.O. Box 5042
Mill Valley 94942

If you go hiking with a group, usually you need not socialize with the others; just remain within sight and sound of them. However, if at any time you leave the group *it is essential* that you notify the leader. He has counted their number, and if he comes up short at the next rest stop, the entire outing may be disrupted while search parties are sent out.

For those persons who like to hike solo or duo, here are a few suggestions:

1. Always leave word with someone where you are going and when you expect to return.

2. Never hitchhike unless you can choose your driver. To illustrate: I would never try to hitch a ride on the highway. However, if I wanted to go from the Five Brooks trailhead to the Bear Valley trailhead without walking five miles, or if it appeared that the #65 Golden Gate Transit bus was so crowded I'd have to stand up from Olema to San Anselmo, then I might ask a ride from a safe-looking car—preferably a family with young children, or a group of middle-aged women.

If you try to hitch rides, don't be surprised or offended when you get turned down—especially if you are a male—and don't take it personally.

We live, alas, in a world where we cannot depend on the kindness of strangers.

3. Corollary to 2: if you are driving, never pick up hitchhikers on the highway.

4. When you break for lunch, try to choose some place with other people around, such as a popular picnic area, beach or campground.

5. If you are riding Golden Gate Transit, try to avoid transferring at Marin City after dark. During the day on weekends a thriving flea market adjoins the bus stop and there are hundreds of people around, but at night the place is isolated and deserted. (A friend of mine nearly got mugged here by a group of juveniles one night.) The bus stops at downtown San Anselmo, downtown Sausalito and the toll plaza are much more frequented at night.

# FLOWERS OF POINT REYES

On the following pages are drawings of some of the flowering plants you are most likely to see in Point Reyes National Seashore. The selection includes a few plants that are not native to the area but, once introduced here, have flourished sufficiently to become extremely common (e.g., the aggressive and pesty milk thistle). The plants are arranged roughly by color of flower to aid in identifying them.

This selection gives only a tiny hint of the plentiful and diverse flora of the National Seashore.

(The drawings are by Jeanne R. Janish, from the book, Flowers of Point Reyes National Seashore, by Roxana S. Ferris. They are reproduced here by courtesy of the University of California Press.)

Indian paintbrush - *Castilleja franciscana*

Blue blossom - *Ceanothus thyrsiflorus*

Annual lupine - *Lupinus bicolor*

Baby-blue-eyes - *Nemophila menziesii*

Ithuriel's spear - *Brodiaea laxa*

93

Dwarf brodiaea - *Brodiaea coronaria*

Blue dicks, or wild hyacinth - *Brodiaea pulchella*

Douglas iris - *Iris douglasiana*

Blue-eyed grass - *Sisyrinchium bellum*

Coast fiddleneck - *Amsinckia spectabilis*

Wild mustard - *Brassica kaber*

Sun cups - *Camissonia ovata*

Scotch broom - *Cystisus scoparius*

Seaside woolly sunflower, or Lizardtail - *Eriophyllum staechadifolium*

Gumplant - *Grindelia stricta venulosa*

Tidy tips - *Layia platyglossa*

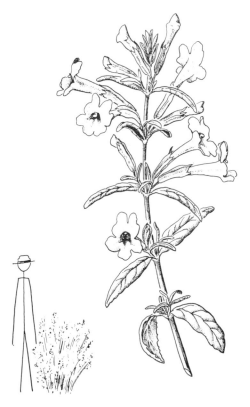

Sticky monkey-flower - *Mimulus aurantiacus*

99

Godetia, or Farewell-to-spring - *Clarkia amoena*

Seaside daisy - *Erigeron glaucus*

Yerba santa - *Eriodictyon californicum*

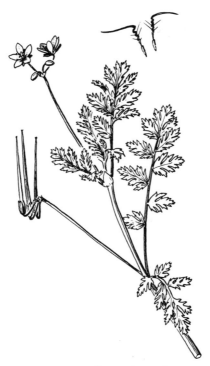

Filaree - *Erodium cicutarium*

Flowering currant - *Ribes sanguineum glutinosum*

Salmonberry - *Rubus spectabilis franciscanum*

Wild hollyhock, or Checkerbloom - *Sidalcea malvaeflora*

Milk thistle - *Silybum marianum*

Hedge-nettle - *Stachys rigida quercetorum*

Bolinas manzanita - *Arctostaphylos virgata*

Coyote bush, or coyote brush - *Baccharis pilularis consanguinea*

Field chickweed - *Cerastium arvense*

105

Poison hemlock - *Conium maculatum*

Coast buckwheat - *Eriogonum latifolium*

Salal - *Gaultheria shallon*

Cow parsnip - *Heracleum lanatum*

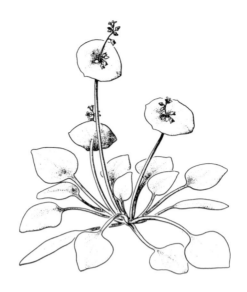

Miner's lettuce - *Montia perfoliata*

Thimbleberry - *Rubus parviflorus*

Blackberry - *Rubus ursinus*

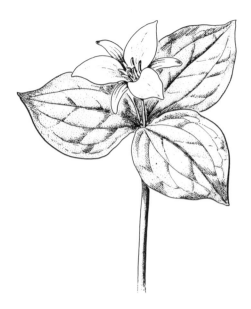

Western trillium, or Wake robin - *Trillium ovatum*

California huckleberry - *Vaccinium ovatum*

# 1991 Supplement

**p. 16, col. 2, paragraph 2:** In the past decade one animal has progressed from being a mere annoyance to an actual danger: the Western black-legged tick. A small percentage of these ticks—probably less than five per cent—carry the spirochete that causes Lyme disease (named for Old Lyme, Connecticut, where it was first diagnosed in 1975). Symptoms can include a red, circular rash and/or a fever, followed by neurological and/or cardiac problems and arthritislike joint pains. Drugs are effective against Lyme disease once it is correctly diagnosed.

The best way to avoid Lyme disease is to avoid ticks. Apply insect repellent before going outdoors. Wear light-colored clothing so that ticks will be more easily visible; wear long sleeves and long pants. Because ticks generally travel *upward,* tuck pants into socks and tuck shirts into pants. If you find a tick on you, try to get someone else to remove it with tweezers as soon as possible.

Recommended reading: Drummond, Roger, *Ticks and What You Can Do About Them.* Berkeley: Wilderness Press, 1990.

**p. 17, col. 1, paragraph 6:** Great white sharks continue to be a hazard; in fact, *San Francisco Examiner* writer Tom Stienstra has dubbed the Bay Area coast the shark attack capital of the world.

**p. 17, Recommended reading:** Evens, Jules G., *The Natural History of the Point Reyes Peninsula.* Point Reyes: Point Reyes National Seashore Association, 1988.

**p. 21, col. 1, paragraph 3:** On September 28, 1985, the 24,000-acre designated wilderness area of the Point Reyes National Seashore was officially dedicated to Congressman Phillip Burton, who had died in 1983. Burton, Representative from San Francisco since 1964, was responsible for more than doubling the wilderness acreage in the national-park system. Congress chose Point Reyes to commemorate Burton because it was the wilderness area closest to his home.

Visitors to the National Seashore will occasionally come across plaques noting that certain facilities—e.g., the Bear Valley Visitor Center—were made possible with the help of a grant from the San Francisco Foundation. These reflect one of the more bizarre chapters in the history of organized philanthropy.

In 1975 Beryl Buck, a childless widow, died and in her will specified that the yearly earnings from her estate were to be used "for exclusively nonprofit, charitable, religious or educational purposes in providing care for the needy of Marin, and for other nonprofit charitable, religious or educational purposes of that county." To administer it Mrs. Buck appointed the San Francisco Foundation, a hitherto low-key institution accustomed to distributing philanthropic monies around the Bay Area. By the time her estate was settled, her original bequest of a comparatively modest $7 million in oil stock had ballooned to over $250 million, meaning that the San Francisco Foundation now had $20 million or more to distribute every year in what was already one of the wealthiest counties in California.

The San Francisco Foundation, abetted by a group of public-interest lawyers representing other Bay Area charities, petitioned to break the "Marin-only" feature of Mrs. Buck's will. They were opposed by the Marin Board of Supervisors, the Marin Council of Agencies, and Mrs. Buck's attorney. The resulting bitter court fight was dubbed "The Superbowl of Probate".

Ultimately the San Francisco Foundation not only had to give up its attempt to break Mrs. Buck's will, but also agreed to turn over the giant trust to a new Marin-based foundation. Ironically enough, over $10 million of Mrs. Buck's estate—which, remember, was originally intended for the "needy of Marin"— went to lawyers for both sides.

**p. 23, How To Get There By Car:** In the summer of 1988 the California Department of Transportation (Caltrans) began double-striping roads in West Marin, making it illegal for cars to pass one another on the double-striped sections. This action was the result of a 10-year-old federal order—originally intended as a safety measure—to forbid passing on all two-lane rural highways with visibility of less than a thousand feet. California was the last state to comply with the rule, but finally had to give in under the threat that otherwise the federal government would withhold all highway funds. Caltrans correctly foresaw that residents of rural areas like Big Sur and West Marin would be furious when they found mile after mile of their roads double-striped, with few turnouts. The net result of this supposed safety measure may be *more* accidents, as frustrated drivers caught behind slow-moving vehicles and finding no legal place to pass will dash across the lines into an unsafe place. An immediate result of double-striping Highway 1 in Marin was to make illegal the Bolinas-Stinson Beach school bus, as well as the large Muir Woods tourist buses—all of which had to cross the center lines on sharp turns.

Eventually all the access roads to the National Seashore may be double-striped for most of their length. Visitors driving in the area should bear in mind:

1. The fine for crossing a double line is $81 on the first offense;

2. California law requires any slower-moving vehicle closely followed by five or more other vehicles to pull over at the first opportunity.

Early in 1990 a landslide—possibly a delayed result of the Loma Prieta earthquake of October 1989—closed part of Highway 1 about halfway between Muir Beach and Stinson Beach. As this goes to press it is still closed, and travelers must use Panoramic Highway to reach Stinson Beach and points north. For an update on the situation, phone the Highway Condition Information recording at 557-3755.

**p. 23, Within the Park:** As whale watching has become ever more popular, the NPS has reinstituted shuttle-bus service on winter weekends.

**p. 23, Facilities:**

### Additional Seashore phone number

663-9029 gives a recorded message about the day's weather, campsite availability and whale visibility.

### New radio information

The Seashore broadcasts park information on AM1610; tune in your car radio when driving on Bear Valley Road or towards the lighthouse.

### Facilities for the disabled

The National Park Service and the Point Reyes National Seashore Association, in the park's quarterly newsletter for Fall 1988, state:

> On-going efforts are being made to include disabled visitors to all buildings and programs. A copy of the Point Reyes National Seashore accessibility guide is available free from any of the park's visitor centers. The NPS provides a wheelchair for

temporary use by park visitors. No rental fee is charged. The wheelchair is available at the Bear Valley Visitor Center.

The Earthquake Trail (see p. 31) is entirely wheelchair-accessible.

**p. 24, col. 2, paragraph 2:** Reservations for campsites may be made by phoning Bear Valley headquarters (663-1092) between 9 A.M. and noon, Monday through Friday.

**p. 24, Hostel:** The current phone number of the Point Reyes Hostel is 663-8811. The current phone number of American Youth Hostels' Golden Gate Council is 863-9939.

**p. 25, Horses:** Bear Valley Stables no longer rents horses, but Five Brooks Stables leads trail rides. Reservations are advisable for weekends; phone 663-1570.

**p. 25, Llamas:** Camelid Capers is a company that provides pack llamas for day trips in the National Seashore (phone 669-1523).

**p. 25, Educational Programs:** The Point Reyes National Seashore Association has taken over the activities formerly administered by the Coastal Parks Association, and sponsors the extensive educational program of the Point Reyes Field Seminars.

The new Clem Miller Environmental Educational Center opened early in 1987, replacing the former one, which had been based in a World War II quonset hut. (The center is named for the Marin Representative who was killed in an airplane accident in 1962, shortly after he had steered through Congress the legislation establishing the National Seashore.) The new center, which took more than two years and almost a half million dollars to plan and construct, was financed through private donations, including those of the William Field Charitable Fund and the Buck Fund.

**p. 25, Hiking Groups, Current Addresses and Phone Numbers:**

Golden Gate Audubon Society, Inc.
1250 Addison Street, #107B
Berkeley 94702
phone: 843-2222

Marin Audubon Society
Box 599
Mill Valley 94942

California Native Plant Society
909 Twelfth Street, Suite 116
Sacramento 95814
phone: (916) 447-2677

Sierra Club, San Francisco Bay Chapter
6014 College Avenue
Oakland 94618
phone: 653-6127

Sierra Club, Marin Group
c/o San Francisco Bay Chapter

**p. 26, Dogs:** Dogs are no longer allowed at Abbotts Lagoon because it is a prime nesting area for many birds, including an endangered species, the snowy plover. Headquarters issues a free list of dog rules for the Seashore and the GGNRA.

**p. 26, Bicycles:** In the fall of 1984, NPS headquarters in Washington ruled that a clause in the 1964 Federal Wilderness Act barring all forms of "mechanical transport" in the wilderness areas applied to bicycles. This ruling may have resulted from the advent and immediate popularity of mountain bikes capable of running over rough terrain. In any event, it led to some highly charged meetings of the Citizens' Advisory Commission for the GGNRA and Point Reyes. Bicycle enthusiasts pointed out that the 24,000 acres of the National Seashore designated as wilderness include some of the trails that have traditionally been most popular with bicyclists, such as the southern ¾ mile of the Bear Valley Trail.

As this goes to press, the ruling still stands. Headquarters issues maps showing permissible bike routes.

The NPS has posted the following rules for mountain bikes:

- Maximum speed 15 miles per hour;
- when visibility is less than 50 feet, slow to walking speed;
- stay on trails;
- alert trail users ahead of you of your approach.

Bicycles can be rented at Point Reyes Bikes, 11431 Highway 1, Point Reyes Station; phone 663-1768; open 10–6 daily except Tuesday.

Trailhead Rentals in Olema rents bikes, cameras, tents, binoculars and other gear; phone 663-1958; open 9:30–6:30.

**p. 27, Nearby Towns:** Bed-and-breakfastry seems to be the leading growth industry in West Marin. To find out about these places, you can phone:

Bed and Breakfast Cottages of Point Reyes 927-9445

Coastal Lodging of West Marin 663-1351

The Inns of Point Reyes 663-1420

**p. 27, Olema:** The Olema Inn has closed and reopened more than once since the first edition of this book came out. As this Supplement goes to press, it is open (phone 663-9559).

**p. 27, Inverness:** Jack Mason, who devoted the latter part of his life to writing and publishing books about West Marin history—and whom I have quoted frequently throughout this book—died in January 1985. Shortly before his death he willed his house, The Gables, to the Inverness Foundation to function as a museum for his collection of West Marin memorabilia and to house the Inverness public library, which for years operated out of a funky one-room building no larger than a bookmobile. It was, in fact, the smallest free-standing library in the nation!

With the enthusiastic support of the community—and a grant from the Buck Fund—Mason's Victorian home has been turned into a charming structure housing an enlarged library and a museum containing his invaluable collection of photos, books, manuscripts and artifacts connected with Marin history.

The library/museum is located at 15 Park Way, Inverness, just one block west of Sir Francis Drake Blvd. Hours: Monday, 3–6 P.M. and 7–9 P.M.; Tuesday and Wednesday, 10 A.M. to 1 P.M. and 2–6 P.M.; Friday, 3–6 P.M.; Saturday, 10 A.M. to 1 P.M.; phone 669-1288.

**p. 28, col. 1, paragraph 3:** Some Bolinas citizens go on removing every road sign to their town that Caltrans erects on Highway 1. They have thereby gained for Bolinas notoriety in such national publications as the *Wall Street Journal* and the *New York Times*.

**p. 31, Earthquake Trail:** The Loma Prieta quake of October 17, 1989, which caused so much damage elsewhere in the Bay Area, had relatively little effect on Point Reyes.

**p. 46, col. 1, paragraph 4:** The Beatty Trail is permanently closed.

**p. 51, col. 1, paragraph 4:** The new Clem Miller Environmental Education Center opened in 1987; see note above for p. 25.

**p. 71, Regulations:** $5 day-use fee per car, $4 for seniors; backpack/bicycle campsites $3 per person per night. Park open 8 A.M. to sunset; all cars must leave by sunset.

**p. 73, Abbotts Lagoon Regulations:** Dogs are no longer allowed at Abbotts Lagoon because it is a prime nesting area for many birds, including an endangered species, the snowy plover.

**p. 68, col. 2, paragraph 1:** Part of the Pierce Ranch has been renovated and a wheelchair-accessible, self-guided tour installed.

**p. 76, col. 2, paragraph 1:** See preceding note.

### p. 88, Current addresses of Sierra Club:

National Headquarters
730 Polk Street
San Francisco 94109
phone: 776-2211

San Francisco Bay Chapter
6014 College Avenue
Oakland 94618
phone: 653-6127

Marin County Regional Group
c/o San Francisco Bay Chapter